Now That We Are Free

Published in association with the
Institute for Democracy in South Africa

Now That We Are Free

Coloured Communities
in a Democratic South Africa

edited by
Wilmot James, Daria Caliguire, and Kerry Cullinan

assisted by
Janet Levy and Shauna Westcott

LYNNE
RIENNER
PUBLISHERS

BOULDER
LONDON

All photographs by Eric Miller

Published in the United States of America in 1996 by
Lynne Rienner Publishers, Inc.
1800 30th Street, Boulder, Colorado 80301

and in the United Kingdom by
Lynne Rienner Publishers, Inc.
3 Henrietta Street, Covent Garden, London WC2E 8LU

ISBN: 1-55587-693-5

Library of Congress Cataloging-in-Publication Data
A Cataloging-in-Publication record for this book
is available from the Library of Congress.

British Cataloguing in Publication Data
A Cataloguing in Publication record for this book
is available from the British Library.

Printed and bound in the United States of America

The paper used in this publication meets the requirements
of the American National Standard for Permanence
of Paper for Printed Library Materials Z39.48-1984.

5 4 3 2 1

Contents

Now That We Are Free

Introduction

Wilmot James
Executive Director
Institute for Democracy in South Africa

Daria Caliguire
Researcher
Institute for Democracy in South Africa

In August 1995, the Institute for Democracy in South Africa (Idasa) held a conference entitled "National Unity and the Politics of Diversity: The Case of the Western Cape". The title reveals a number of concerns Idasa had about the participation of the people of the Western Cape, particularly the coloured communities, in the nation-building project launched by the government of national unity after the elections of April 1994.

This is not to say that other communities in South Africa – for example, people of Indian or Venda origin – do not show similar features of marginalisation from the nation-building project. Marginality is not necessarily imbued with an ethnic quality at every turn: sectors of rural and urban South Africa across the racial and ethnic spectrum feel distant from the political centre that drives the nation-building project.

But, in tackling the topic, Idasa had to start somewhere and thus chose the Western Cape, with the focus on the coloured communities. In preparation for the conference we ran four community-based workshops in urban and rural Western Cape. In the process we encountered on a regular basis cynicism, scepticism and doubt about the benefits brought by our new democracy. Grievances ranged from feeling left out, being dealt poor treatment and being bumped out of the queue for anticipated state benefits.

The conference was designed as a space and an opportunity to voice and to hear the many varied political expressions of grievance, to get a better grasp of the issues residing behind some of the racial tensions in the province, and to begin to define some answers to problems raised. This book is an edited collection of the proceedings. All the papers, save that of Yunus Carrim, were presented in one form or another at the conference.

Participants to the conference had the considerable honour of an opening address by President Nelson Mandela. His speech is reproduced here as the first chapter in the section outlining

1

the context in which the conference took place. The president's presence indicated his concern and interest in the affairs of the Western Cape, particularly the disaffection in some coloured communities and misperceptions about what his government is trying to accomplish. We were gratified by his remarks.

On the basis of the four community workshops and one research workshop, we commissioned Mark Kaplan of Intermedia to produce a video to capture the areas of racial conflict that have emerged since the 1994 elections, as well as the views of some critical personalities in the debate. The video, entitled "Now That We are Free", was shown at the conference as a somewhat rude introduction to the scope of problems in the Western Cape and the potential for conflict if matters remain unresolved. In the second chapter, Daria Caliguire reflects on the thematic issues raised by the workshops and the video and allow the voices of the communities to filter through as a scene-setter for the chapters that follow.

The third chapter also aims to provide a context for the analysis in subsequent sections, by addressing the burning issue of gangsterism in the Cape Flats. This is a particular pathology, due in part to the legacy of apartheid, which threatens the social fabric of coloured communities in this time of transition. Irvin Kinnes re-frames traditional thinking on the problem of gangsterism in a way that facilitates broad, community-based solutions.

The second section provides a spread of interpretations of the coloured vote in the country's first democratic elections. The various contributions by Brian Williams, Jeremy Seekings and Wilmot James provide readings of the election outcome that differ from the conventional wisdom which maintains that the coloured vote was a racial census of sorts. Yunus Carrim's chapter was not presented at the conference, but is included in the book because of his interesting comparisons between the Indian vote and the coloured vote as distinct cases of "minority" electoral participation in the elections.

The third section deals with identity questions. During the conference proceedings, coloured communities' search for identity emerged as a critical step in a larger process of carving out political space for participation. Ebrahim Rasool, Peter Marais and Julian Sonn examine the construction of identity in racial terms, specifically with reference to the coloured people, and its implications for the creation of a non-racial society and state.

The fourth section considers affirmative action and equity. In an attempt to understand rising tensions between some segments of coloured and African communities in the Western Cape, affirmative action as a means for achieving equity is examined within a framework that recognises the historical linkages between race and access to resources in this country. Howard Gabriels, Mamphela Ramphele and Philip Black and Valerie Flanagan recontextualise affirmative action with respect to public and private sector notions of the policy and how these translate into practice.

The fifth section revisits the concept of non-racialism as an approach to politics. Although the concept is initially examined with reference to the coloured communities of the Western Cape, the analysis soon transcends any regional specificity to speak with greater relevance to the overarching national question: in a society of divided communities, what does it mean to construct a national identity? Furthermore, how can the individual interests of distinct racial or ethnic communities be served without endangering the broader enterprise of creating and managing national unity? The contributions by Hermann Giliomee, Barbara Masekela and Neville Alexander attempt to answer these questions from a broad range of perspectives.

The sixth part brings to bear some comparative views, drawing on the experiences of Canada, Britain, Brazil and Malaysia, on the management of racial and ethnic diversity. The conclusion provides a second approximation of the issues and outlines a programme of action.

For the sake of clarity, we have been forced to use racial categories in some instances. However, the term black is used to refer to all those discriminated against by apartheid, namely African, coloured and Indian people.

We would like to acknowledge the role played by Derrick Marco of Idasa's Western Cape office in the running of the community-based and research workshops. We received valuable advice and direction from Mamphela Ramphele, Neville Alexander, Barney Pityana, David Schmidt and Brian Williams, who acted as a reference group for the conference planners. The organisation of the conference was ably executed by Beverley Haubrich.

Idasa would also like to acknowledge our funders. The Friedrich Naumann Stiftung, represented by Gottfried Wüst and Bettina Braemer, was our main funder and is also a co-publisher of this book. The Royal Netherlands Embassy made a substantial contribution, while additional support was received from the United States Information Service and the British Council.

Finally, Mamphela Ramphele's chapter, "Treading the thorny path to equity", appears in Ramphele, M (1995) *The Affirmative Action Book* (Cape Town : Idasa). ▲

This book explains the topics discussed in workshops. The workshops were somewhat of a brain-storming session to bring out problems & by so doing, finding solutions to these problems.

Section 1

The Context

President Nelson Mandela

Chapter 1

Citizens of a single rainbow nation

Mandela encourages the people to speak up & be heard. Only by defining problems, can people find solutions.

Nelson Mandela
President of South Africa

Racism is a national problem in search of a national solution. And we are right to look forward to a future in which we shall have South African communities in our residential areas; not racial groups closeted in racially-defined "group areas".

One of South Africa's most valuable assets is the vibrant civil society forged by its people in the struggle for freedom. It is on the continued vibrancy of this civil society that the future of our democracy depends.

I am therefore most honoured to share in your conference, all the more because I know that my presence here does not signify any relaxation of your vigilance in monitoring the actions of government.

Idasa's contribution to democracy in South Africa is a distinguished one, marked by a readiness to confront challenging situations. This is vividly expressed in the theme for this Western Cape conference. It is right to confront the difficult issues that our divisive history has posed for the community which forms most of this province's population. Idasa does the cause of nation building service by laying bare for frank discourse issues that many would prefer to whisper in corridors.

It is right to speak out.

Countless individuals, of all colours and backgrounds, have contributed to South Africa's attainment of liberty, justice and democracy. Many are from the coloured community, which has

6

nurtured a long tradition of struggle against oppression. This community has given our nation outstanding leaders whose contribution and sacrifice for the ideal of a non-racial democracy has been immense.

In the past they helped shape resistance politics, through each of its phases. Today they represent our nation as a whole, in parliament and provincial governments, leading the transformation of our society.

Our newly established democracy is the culmination of decades of struggle and the beginning of an era of hope and promise. The particular abuses under apartheid laws which the coloured community suffered – the Group Areas and Mixed Marriages Acts in particular – are things of the past. Under our democratic Constitution all South Africans enjoy the right to be protected and not abused by the law. *Giving encouragement, trying to settle the people's fears*

But still a long way to go!

South Africa shall never repeat the horrific abuses of detention without trial. Never again will our nation be at war with itself. Imam Haron, Basil February and Ashley Kriel will be remembered as towering monuments of this, our commitment.

Freedom, justice and fairness are the ideals we must strive to fully realise. But already all our people, from whatever sector, feel the dignity and pride of a nation which freed itself in the elections last year. Non-racialism is one of those ideals that unites us. It recognises South Africans as citizens of a single rainbow nation, acknowledging and appreciating difference and diversity.

Turning ideal into living reality will require, among other things, undoing the consequences of discriminatory practices of the past, in particular in employment and education. Affirmative action is a strategy of corrective action to bring previously disadvantaged people up to the same competitive levels as those people who have been advantaged.

speaks of the benefits of affirm action

This policy has awakened fears among sections of the coloured community. It is sometimes said to be intended to benefit only Africans, and there are claims that a few employers misinterpret it in this way.

It is necessary therefore to repeat categorically that anyone who says affirmative action reserves jobs or opportunities for Africans only is grossly distorting the policy of the government and the African National Congress. Anyone denied an opening in this way is denied a right that belongs to all who have been disadvantaged, and they should take it up with the authorities.

The Reconstruction and Development Programme (RDP) is sometimes the subject of similar false claims. But a look at the facts shows that the Presidential Lead Projects and RDP forums have generated a range of projects in Cape Town and the rural areas of the Western Cape, too many to detail here. They bring direct and indirect benefits for the coloured community.

briefly dis- cusses positive steps forward toward equality

Having said that, we need to do more. One of the main obstacles to systematic progress and proper involvement of communities in the RDP has been the absence of democratic local authorities. In this regard the local government elections are of critical importance. Democratic local authorities will help us to join hands to heal the social fabric of our communities, damaged by the enforced divisions of apartheid. *Community – work toward ending apartheid.* The government has already urged an end to racism in the workplace. But we need to go further. We need, as a nation, to strenuously combat racism wherever it raises its ugly head.

Chap. 3 discusses police corruption

There are those who say that some coloured people have not yet entered the new South Africa and that they are prone to using racist language encouraged under apartheid. Where this may be true, we should emphasise that it is not unique to sections of the coloured community. Racism is

Continues to stress "we," "community," "as a nation"

7

[handwritten left margin: racism continues due to separation in living areas began by apartheid.]

found in all spheres of our society. This is aggravated by the fact that we have inherited a society in which racism is configured with geometric precision in the maps of our residential areas.

Racism is a national problem in search of a national solution. And we are right to look forward to a future in which we shall have South African communities in our residential areas; not racial groups closeted in racially-defined "group areas". *[handwritten: In the future, no such thing as group areas]* De-racialising South African society is the new moral and political challenge facing our young democracy, and it is one that we should grapple with decisively. We need to marshal our resources in a visible campaign to combat racism – in the workplace, in our schools, in the residential areas and in all aspects of our public life. *[handwritten: Building steam]*

I use the word "campaign" advisedly. As with all our goals, de-racialising our society requires active co-operation between government and civil society, including non-governmental organisations and voluntary associations.

It is understandable that each sector of South African society should have concerns unique to its history and circumstances. For some within the coloured community, perhaps the most pressing concern is the fear of being marginalised.

[handwritten margin: XX] If left unattended, this fear could undermine the very foundation of non-racial democracy that we all have struggled to achieve. If parties which seek to encourage and exploit this are not challenged, they will succeed in perpetuating the divisions of the past. *[handwritten: Must not be fearful of challenging what is wrong.]*

We have favourable conditions for dealing with these anxieties. One year since the elections brought democracy, it is feasible to make a more realistic assessment of what the transformation in our society means. Those who prophesied doom and an early end to reconciliation have been proved wrong. The benefits of the democratic order have become more tangible.

What is called for is a strengthening of the developing partnership among all communities, in the spirit of reconciliation and renewal.

*[handwritten margin: * Eases their fears.]* For its part, government is committed to an unqualified observance of the principles of non-racialism and equality. We are clear about our goals and plans and shall always be sensitive to the apprehensions any section of our people may feel.

For the coloured community, as with every other community in our varied land, it means becoming part of the majority by embracing our new society. It means building our South African nation and a better life for all.

In the past, the issues on which Idasa concentrated our minds had great significance for the future nation. We are convinced that this is the case today and that the organisation shall always carry this banner. May delegates here fare well in their deliberations. And may Idasa continue to challenge us in public office. *[handwritten: ▲ Welcomes challenges because they ✱ bring about positive changes.]*

[handwritten: He never say "I," he always says "We",....]

Chapter 2

Voices from the communities

Daria Caliguire
Researcher
Institute for Democracy in South Africa

"It is interesting that we have these conflicts in the Western Cape between the coloureds and the (African) communities because we were one nation ... It was unfortunate that the system, the previous government, had to remove this from us."

The April 1994 elections marked the beginning of a period of dramatic change in South Africa – a long-awaited shift from the authoritarianism of the old apartheid regime to the new, inclusive democracy of the government of national unity. But the transition to democracy has brought with it a degree of uncertainty as political space has been opened up for individuals and communities to renegotiate and redefine their own place as well as their relations to one another in the new democratic map of this country.

This feeling of uncertainty seems to be particularly pronounced within the coloured communities of South Africa. In order to gain a ground-level understanding of the sources, nature and extent of this feeling, Idasa conducted a series of interviews which culminated in community-based workshops in the Western Cape at Grabouw, Mossel Bay, Heinz Park and the University of the Western Cape. These provide the raw material used to feel "the pulse" of coloured communities and, where they are neighbours, the perspective from African communities. The voices in this chapter are representative of those articulated in the workshop process. Taken together, they reveal the range of issues facing coloured communities and of positions taken by such communities.

In some sectors, a sense of insecurity has translated into an increasing politicisation and mobilisation of racial identity as a way of securing a political place. In 1995, the growing number of coloured political formations, some of which make secessionist claims, gives testimony to the extent of disaffection and insecurity among certain segments of the coloured communities. Mervyn Ross of the Kleurling Weerstandsbeweging (KWB) gives voice to this movement at its extreme:

> We are proud that we are ethnic. And once we are ethnic and being recognised by various other people, we can also go further and say, "Look, we are ethnic. We have our own language, our own culture, our own land and we want to govern ourselves." We are not prepared to be governed by the white man anymore – he has made a mess of it for 300 years. We are not prepared to be governed by black people.

Search for identity

One way of understanding the rise of coloured political groupings and movements is as a collective search for identity. Whereas apartheid imposed a definition of coloured in the past, today the question of coloured identity is undergoing a process of rigorous self-examination. For Father Michael Weder, the search for identity is an intensely personal one, and therefore is only legitimate when self-imposed: *No one else can tell you who you are though they may try.*

> It is about who I am. Growing up in 40th Street in Elsie's River, my first identity of who I was was an Anglican at St Andrew's Church, Eureka Estate, and Father Mark was an *umfundisi* (priest) there. But I was also reminded that I was living in the back quarters, the servants' quarters, of Mrs Singh's, a coloured woman married to an Indian businessman. And my Indian brothers reminded me that I was a *boesman*. And my coloured brothers reminded me that I was a *coolie-boesman*. I ultimately had to make the choice about who I was, and I decided I was a Christian. That was my first formative identity. Later on I discovered black consciousness, and it was part of my healing. I later realised it was not the only aspect of my identity: it is actually much broader. But it is a question of choice, of who will decide.

Beyond the quest on an individual level, a collective search for identity on behalf of coloured communities at this point seems to commence with a reclaiming of the past. Weder goes on to illustrate:

> Father McBride reminds us of when as a child his grandfather used to celebrate the 8th of December, and I said, "Father, why the 8th of December as a holiday?" And he said, "That's the day our people were freed as slaves." That date is not on our calendar; it is not an event. But part of our identity lies in those early days and that is where we must start recovering our identity as we become part of the nation.

As opposed to reclaiming the past, the search for identity runs the risk of carrying forward with it much baggage inherited from the past. As Helen le Mark of Mossel Bay explains, for some people the process is still steeped in the thinking and structures of the past:

> I'm a coloured. I was born a coloured. I look back at the old apartheid. Look, apartheid is still there; it is alive and kicking. We cannot think that because De Klerk made that speech in 1990 that it is gone – it is people's attitudes. And because we are in transition and change, people are clinging to that which they still know. So we are still seeing ourselves as coloureds in the old South Africa. That is why we have this KWB who feel: "Look, nobody is accepting us. We're non-blacks and we're non-whites. So let's then search for our identity." Again, I say it is the security within – knowing who you are, where you are going. Coloured people want to be coloured – they want to know who they are.

Racism and racial hierarchy

The need within the coloured communities to affirm an identity and to have the security of place that this in turn confers, is a strong common theme. The absence of such certainty of identity coupled with the lack of a secure place in the post-apartheid non-racial dispensation is seen by many, including Hombi Ntshoko of Langa, to be at the root of the tension within the coloured communities:

> Coloureds don't know where they come from. We know where we come from. Whites know where they come from. But these coloureds don't know whether they are black or white. Hence, they feel so threatened.

Such uncertainty is also a source of tension between the coloured and African communities of the Western Cape. Grabouw resident Bettie Chatburn gives voice to these tensions:

> The blacks call us _boesman_, people without an identity. We are last and they rule.

In turn, Ntshoko voices the reciprocal tension within the black community:

> They call us _kaffirs_. They have been calling us _kaffirs_ for I don't know how long. We have been calling them, in revenge, _boesman_. We have been retaliating now.

Current expressions of racism, especially between the coloured and African communities, can best be understood in terms of the legacy of apartheid. The ANC's Johnny Issel, a member of the Western Cape provincial legislature, links racism within sectors of the coloured community to the underlying search for identity:

> Coloured people want to belong. The apartheid system, however, alienated col-
> oured people so seriously that what we today see coming to the fore in all sorts of

divergent ways, even blatant racism for that matter, is in fact an attempt by coloured people to belong. But it is not only coloured people. All sorts of groups in our country today are finding space not only to reassert themselves but to find a place where they can belong; where they can root themselves.

Apartheid also fuelled racist tensions between communities by tying resource distribution to race. Access to resources under apartheid was determined by a community's place in the established racial hierarchy. For the coloured community, this meant an intermediate and somewhat ambiguous position, as David Smith of Mossel Bay explains:

> Originally you've got the whites and they've got everything. And you've got the blacks, who've got virtually nothing. And we as coloureds in the middle – in a certain way were looked after by the previous government. We were not totally excluded. In some instances, we were advantaged, but not like the whites.

In addition to deepening the crisis of identity within the coloured communities, the intermediate position which they inherited has furthered the sense of divide between the coloured and African communities. Under apartheid, the coloureds felt as if they weren't white enough, and according to Helen le Mark:

> Now we are not black enough. There is uncertainty. There is mistrust ... There is also a feeling among coloured people that we were the "haves" in the past and yet we were also discriminated against. So there is that suspicion.

The fear within the coloured communities that the new democratic order will see a reversal of fortunes between the coloured and African communities is well understood within the African community. Joyce Mawu of Langa recognises this fear and the tension which accompanies it:

> The coloured people, they think now that we are going to be above them, like they are always above us. It is not that way: we want to be one nation ... We are not pushing them aside. We have always been sisters and brothers with them. They (are) feeling scared. They think we (are) going for revenge.

With sadness, Grace Qotoyi of Langa exposes the damage and divisiveness apartheid has brought to the relationship between the coloured and African communities:

> It is interesting that we have these conflicts in the Western Cape between the coloureds and the (African) communities because we were one nation. For instance, I was born in Kensington, and from Kensington we moved to Athlone and we stayed with the coloureds. The way we grew up and the way we were socialised, coloured communities and (African) communities, we were one nation. We were sisters and brothers. It was unfortunate that the system, the previous government, had to remove this from us.

Conflict over resources

The critical link established in the past between race and access to resources continues to operate today. In this period of democratic transition, it threatens to erode a sense of security within certain sectors of the coloured communities. According to Faldeilah de Vries of Manenberg:

> Our community is now in a chaotic phase, and I don't think we can dismiss our history that has brought about this chaos. And I don't think it just has to do with racism. It is also a lack of resources that was created by our history. And therefore, there is a scrambling for housing and land which hasn't been developed over many years, and obviously which cannot be rectified overnight.

The "scrambling" for housing, land and jobs in the present context of delayed RDP implementation adds an edge to the existing tensions between the coloured and African communities. Such an edge provides additional fuel for more separatist interests. Ross of the KWB claims:

> Coloured people don't get houses now. Houses are for the settlers along the N2.[1] Our people are still homeless. Our people are unemployed. There are no jobs for us. We see the money coming in from overseas, pouring into the RDP and it is going to black organisations and businesses.

Issel provides perspective on the current conflict over resource distribution within the broader black community by drawing a silent comparison with access to resources within the white community:

> Our people, black people, oppressed people, have never before been in line to receive. There is a dogfight over the measly delivery efforts. One sees it even within coloured communities – different groups fighting over the few bones that have become available.

A poignant illustration of this is provided by the ongoing conflict in Grabouw over a piece of vacant land called Melrose Place, which is claimed for housing development by both the coloured informal settlement of Snake Park and the African informal settlement of Rooidakke. While the vast majority of land in Grabouw remains securely in the hands of white farmers, the dispossessed African and coloured communities look to Melrose Place as the only opportunity for better housing. The African community, for example, lives in a squatter camp that lacks the most basic facilities: many residents have neither taps nor toilets and feel that the municipality is ignoring their needs.

With two communities in dire need, the battle for Melrose Place gets fought in terms of seniority and tenure, which exacerbates racial tensions. Local Pan Africanist Congress (PAC) leader Dennis Marinus claims that the coloured community in Grabouw has an historical right to Melrose Place, and pledges to continue the fight on that basis:

> People who have lived in Grabouw the longest should be given priority as regards

land ... The people will come back to Melrose Place, no matter what, because they believe that this is their land. The people have waited 20 to 30 years and they are not prepared to wait any longer.

Such conflicts over resources – particularly land and housing – between impoverished coloured and African communities are not unique to Grabouw, but can be found throughout the Western Cape. Other recent examples include the occupation by African people of houses designated for coloured people in Tafelsig (Mitchells Plain) and the clash between coloured residents of Manenberg with African people who had marched to Goodwood to demand a vacant piece of land in Manenberg.

The conflict over resources extends beyond housing and land to employment where the policy of affirmative action is a source of debate. Within certain coloured circles, a common perception that has currency is the belief that affirmative action is disproportionately advantaging Africans at the expense of coloureds. In Mossel Bay, Victor Daniels describes this perception from the perspective of coloured communities:

> More and more you hear about the availability of posts and black people filling them. The people doing the interviews are looking for black people, and not coloured people, but they won't say it, you see. It's like something unwritten – it is not in black and white. But it is there, and the feeling is there in the coloured community as well. But we must look at how black people were marginalised in the past, and the opportunities they had, and the opportunities coloureds had. Coloureds were marginalised but not as much as the black people.

Florina Serfontein, a founding member of the Forum for the Coloured People of South Africa, echoes concerns about the conflict developing over resources, particularly in relation to jobs. She, and many other coloured people, feel marginalised and left out – not only of resource distribution, but the larger political process as well:

> Our people are losing their jobs. Our children can't find work. Wherever you go, if you are not Xhosa speaking, people will not employ you. And I can say it is something that is bugging our people because we are not being heard and that is what we want to see. We want to be heard. We want to be looked at as South Africans. We are being pushed aside and just being grouped to one side. You hear people saying that if you really go back, we have not struggled. (But) we have been part of the struggle. I myself have been part of the struggle. But no one looks at you as being part of the struggle. I think that is unfair.

The need for space and a voice

There is a palpable sense of marginalisation from the new political system which has the power to create a dangerous distance between the coloured communities and other, particularly African, communities of South Africa. The distance is inherited as part of the divisive legacy of apartheid which tore the social fabric of the black community apart by stratifying communities according to imposed racial categories. The racial hierarchy which was then created furthered the divide by placing coloureds "above" blacks and "below" whites.

The resulting middle ground, which became home for the various coloured communities which were neither black nor white, has become a place where uncertainty and ambiguity dwells. During this transition to democracy, it is a place that seems to be more unstable than before as its inhabitants try to navigate through a crisis of identity fraught with threats of racial polarisation. It is a place that also seems to be shrinking as some of its existing residents feel they are losing ground in the new democratic order. That is, what limited benefits were provided in the past are *somewhat* gone and there is a sense of being excluded from the new resources to be distributed. *like the loss of jobs due to emancip and today, immigrat. in the U.S.*

The challenge for South Africa's nascent democracy is to allow space for the coloured communities to participate in an inclusive and secure way in the unfolding political process. Likewise, the challenge for the emerging coloured communities of South Africa, as they define themselves post-apartheid, is to give voice to their interests, concerns and fears in a way that does not foster racial divides. The need to give space and voice presents an essential challenge to nation building in this country. It is a challenge which must be met. ▲

Endnote

1. Ross is refering to the shacks erected by homeless African people along the N2 freeway outside Cape Town.

The best way to prevent a greater divide between coloureds & Africans is by allowing all to speak out — to discuss their fears, their angers in an open setting. Giving them a voice is most important.

Chapter 3

The struggle for the Cape Flats

Irvin Kinnes
Social Development Officer
National Institute for Crime Prevention and Rehabiliation of Offenders

Creating a cycle of negative be- havior like what we see in our own disadvantaged neighborhoods or places like Harlem.

Among the reasons for the high incidence of gangsterism on the Cape Flats is the sheer misery of the environment into which families and whole communities were forcibly relo- cated from inner city areas during the apartheid era.

For everyone in South Africa, from the president to the garbage collector, crime is public enemy number one. The battle against crime, advertised in the same way as a bottle of detergent, affects every major sector of society, from business to politics to education: crime even threatens the Reconstruction and Development Programme (RDP). Of course, criminal activity existed in South Africa long before April 1994, but the new focus on crime reflects both a concern at its prolifera- tion and a shift of energies to address it. *＊Crime is a snowball effect & difficult to stop*

Crime has assumed different features in different parts of the country. In KwaZulu-Natal, it is associated with political violence; in the Eastern Cape, the major problem is violence associated with the taxi industry; in Gauteng, robbery and vehicle hijackings constitute the most problem- atic form of crime; in the Western Cape, crime is associated in the main with gangsterism.

Since the April 1994 elections, there has been a proliferation of gang fights in the Western Cape. In addition to the escalating battle for control of turf in relation to the drugs and arms market, the changing political environment has played a role in this increase in criminal activity. In the run-up to the elections, gangs sought a role in the political process, prompted, on the one hand, by fears of losing ground and, on the other, by eagerness to cash in on opportunities offered by the disorder that the grievances of the white right wing and the Inkatha Freedom Party seemed to portend.

The statistics shown in Table 3.1 tell their own story. Supplied by the South African Police Services (SAPS) Gang Information Unit, the figures reflect the incidence of reported gang fights, murder, attempted murder and robbery for the six-month period of January to July 1995 in the following areas of the Western Cape: Philippi, Bishop Lavis, Bellville South, Manenberg, Macassar, Mitchells Plain, Steenberg, Elsies River, Athlone, Kalksteenfontein and Grassy Park. It is important to remember that the figures reflect only the number of reported gang fights; their actual incidence could be much higher.

Table 3.1:

Crime on the Cape Flats, January to July 1995

Period	Gang fights	Murders	Attempted murders	Robberies
Jan	343	6	9	3
Feb	254	20	42	4
March	505	22	37	6
April	327	17	29	3
May	238	5	19	8
June	262	12	10	4
July	97	7	11	5
TOTAL	2026	89	157	33

A further indication of the extent of the problem is the fact that, between 1 October 1994 and 30 March 1995 in the Manenberg area alone, 44 murders were committed, 28 of which (63 percent) were related to gang activity. In Bishop Lavis during the same period, 49 murders were committed, of which 25 (51 percent) were related to gangsterism.

A holistic approach

violence
really
caused

Among the reasons for this high incidence of gangsterism on the Cape Flats is the sheer misery of the environment into which families and whole communities were forcibly relocated from inner city areas during the apartheid era. The double- and triple-storey council flats built to accommo-

environment / congestion / poverty / etc.

date those torn from their roots are ugly and blatantly inadequate from every point of view. Overcrowding and high levels of unemployment and poverty exacerbate the problem and criminality and violence easily emerge as a response to the experienced violence of a heartless system.

Until recently, a holistic view has been absent from traditional state responses to this problem. In practice, a holistic approach would involve joint strategising and co-operation between the departments of justice, safety and security, education, and health and welfare, together with representatives of the communities in which gangs are based.

It has been argued that one of the problems of the existing system is that the government departments involved seek to advance different interests in relation to dealing with offenders. The police interest is to arrest and prosecute them, the department of justice aims to ensure a conviction, while the department of correctional services seeks their early release.

At a recent Police and Prisons Civil Rights Union (Popcru) meeting on the situation at Pollsmoor Prison, it was reported that Pollsmoor is overcrowded by 209 percent and that the inmate to officer ratio is 46:1. In consequence, prison warders fear that health standards in the prison are declining, along with standards of supervision and treatment of inmates, while the incidence of assault, rape, Aids and gang activity is increasing. Moreover, Pollsmoor, like other prisons in the country, is still under the command of conservatives from the old order.

Among the factors that traditionalists with a law and order agenda fail to take into account is the negative impact of a punitive justice system on the recidivism rate. This has been estimated by the National Institute for Crime Prevention and Rehabilitation of Offenders (Nicro) to be in the region of 70 percent. In other words, of every 10 offenders released from prison, seven return.

Secondly, the traditionalists fail to understand the deep-rooted nature of the problem. The people we call gangsters are our brothers, fathers, cousins, uncles and aunts. Hence, support for gang members is very strong in some communities.

"Operation Gangbust", launched recently by Western Cape MEC for Safety and Security Patrick McKenzie, may ironically also have enhanced the image of gangsters as "untouchables" in the eyes of the youth. While criminals were arrested in the operation, the traditionalists enjoyed only a fleeting victory since, within the hour in many cases, violent gangsters were back on the streets, killing, dealing in drugs and subjecting the community to the usual regime of fear.

In fact, the incidence of killing and injury as a result of gang activity rose within the first few weeks of Operation Gangbust. Police put lots of effort into arresting key gang members, only to find that they did not have a case that would stand up in court. Alternatively, dockets disappeared from the prosecutors' offices, or prosecutors were simply outwitted by defence lawyers. This made gang leaders appear to be beyond the reach of the law.

The principal lesson that has emerged from this failed operation is that gang organisation and resources have improved dramatically over the last few years. Rough and ready street or defence gangs have developed into sophisticated crime syndicates.

In consequence, any attempt to understand and deal with the problem of gangsterism must be based on an analysis that takes account of such factors as the type of gang and its quality of leadership, its relation to prison gangs, its infrastructure and economy, recruitment procedure, networks, information gathering processes and its code of discipline. Additional relevant factors are the gang's geographical spread across the Western Cape, its actual and potential community support and the issue of police corruption and complicity.

It is noteworthy that, despite a police investigation into complicity and corruption in 1989

18

[handwritten marginal notes:] Poverty is a strong indicator of crime and, violence often breeds violence

a Joke Gang activity actually rose after Operation Gangbust, often those arrested were quickly released due to lack of evidence

Problem here as well. + Police corruption grew. None found corrupt were fired, only transferred.

Instead of firing corrupt officers, they moved them.

and a subsequent report that received considerable media attention, no significant attempts were made to rid the police force of corrupt officers. They were simply transferred to other areas. *Doesn't solve the problem*

They were finding solutions but not making them public.

Allegations of police corruption surfaced again during the last four months of 1994. McKenzie appointed a one-person commission to advise him on restructuring the police force in the Western Cape and commissioner Perry Anderson made concrete proposals in relation to corruption and the morale of police officers. Why has this report not been made public? Equally, while one must welcome the appointment of a civilian – criminologist Wilfried Scharf – to oversee investigations into allegations of police corruption, one is entitled to ask why no results have been forthcoming when the inquiry has been under way for months.

These are important questions for, despite the new community policing initiative, we have a long way to go in building community trust in the police. Such trust is a vain hope in the absence of openness about the results of investigations.

A new challenge

In relation to the gangs themselves, an issue that needs to be focused on intensively is why young people join gangs. Extensive work with gang members has convinced me that youths join gangs on the Cape Flats mostly as a result of peer pressure and as a defence against a collective feeling of rejection by either their families or sections of the community in which they live. The families *searching for* of many gang members are indigent and youths join the gangs as a means to provide themselves with both material resources and a sense of identity and belonging. There is also a common fear of the future and what it holds. *Same here*

Given this context, it is abundantly clear that the issue of gangsterism, and of crime in general, cannot be addressed in a political and social vacuum. Any attempt at a solution must take into account the very same alienation that coloured people are talking about on the political level. Moreover, political parties should resist the temptation to gain political mileage by professing to be tough on crime and calling for the death penalty. The death penalty has never been a deterrent to violent crime.

The challenge for politicians is to make the RDP work for the communities of the Cape Flats, transform prisons into places where inmates can be productive, and give communities a role in the criminal justice system, particularly in relation to the sentencing of offenders. Dealing with the problem of gangsterism, and crime prevention generally, requires the urgent development of our communities and a concurrent development of positive role models for the youth. Obviously, *way to combat violence* it also requires ongoing efforts to nurture the kind of co-operation between communities and the criminal justice system evident in such initatives as community policing forums, community court assessors, neighbourhood watches and anti-crime forums, which have begun to make it more difficult for criminals to commit crimes. *Can't be done by individuals*

A new challenge awaits us. It beckons us to immediately defend our schools from vandalism and build them into creative centres of learning. It beckons us to rekindle in our communities the moral values of respect for human life and dignity, tolerance of difference, and willingness to share responsibility for the welfare of our society. Let us not be the victors of an hour, but the victors of our future! ▲

Violence blacks against blacks

Making Sense of the Coloured Vote

Chapter 4

The power
of propaganda

Brian Williams
Western Cape Secretary
Metal and Electrical Workers Union of South Africa

Part of the history of the coloured community includes op-
pression and exploitation at the hands of the NP regime.
Many of the community's finest sons and daughters were
jailed or killed in the reign of terror perpetrated in an at-
tempt to prop up apartheid.

Introduction

Given that South Africa's April 1994 elections saw a majority of coloured people voting the National Party (NP) into power in the Western Cape, would it be fair to assume that the coloured community is a problematic one? Had the African National Congress (ANC) won that provincial election, would the topic "National Unity and the Politics of Diversity" have been considered worthy of discussion?

More than a year after that election, it is useful to engage in a debate about South Africa's coloured community a community that, significantly, has yet to free itself from the stranglehold of psychological enslavement. It is appropriate to challenge current social theories about communities and societies and to seek new, alternative explanations for their actions. More particularly, one should confront narrow, elitist notions held about a community, such as the coloured community, that has yet to find and define itself as well as its place in the building of a united nation.

Socially distinct and oppressed

It is not uncommon to hear certain left-wing academics speak of the coloured community as though it were not socially identifiable. They argue that this "community" is no more than a political construction, artificially created by colonialists and agents of imperialism.

On the contrary, I would argue that the coloured community is both socially distinct and diverse. Furthermore, its history is more complex than the above argument allows and the existence of this community is the consequence of many factors. There need be no contradiction to being coloured and South African while at the same time socialist, anti-capitalist and anti-imperialist.

Part of the history of the coloured community includes oppression and exploitation at the hands of the NP regime. Many of the community's finest sons and daughters were jailed or killed in the reign of terror perpetrated in an attempt to defend apartheid.

In pre-1994 elections, the coloured community boycotted undemocratic polls or used its limited franchise to vote against the NP. But in South Africa's first democratic election, a majority of coloured people voted their traditional oppressor into power in the Western Cape provincial elections, leaving many activists and left-wingers stunned.

The reasons for the election result are complex, but paramount is the awesome power of propaganda. The NP, in at least one respect, has confirmed Richard Hyman's (1975: 17) description of power as being "not only the ability to overcome opposition, but the ability to prevent opposition from even arising simply because those subjected to a particular form of control do not question its legitimacy or can see no alternative".

Control through propaganda

According to Johan de Wet (1988: 44), since 1914 propaganda has replaced bribery and force as the main means of enlisting support. He argues that: "Propaganda is a deliberate attempt by some individual or group to form, control or alter the attitudes of other groups by means of communication with the intention that in any given situation the reaction of those so influenced will be that desired by the propagandist".

The popular contemporary perspective of propaganda holds that it is a powerful instrument which can be used to manipulate large numbers of essentially passive people by means of mass persuasion. It works on a psychological level and is directed at groups rather than individuals. French philosopher Jacques Ellul holds that propaganda is pervasive, complete and all encompassing. It would be a mistake to view propaganda in a limited way, used only by certain people for select purposes at certain convenient times.

It is by recognising propaganda as a sociological phenomenon that we can begin to make sense of the coloured vote in the 1994 Western Cape election. Also at issue are the ANC's communication and election strategies.

The NP won because the ANC failed to understand the socio-economic, cultural and political realities of the Western Cape *and* because the ANC ignored the NP's oppressive past. The ANC focused on the future and the benefits of a new government while making vague political promises. It did not seek to expose the NP for what it was and what it had done to the people of the Western Cape, especially the coloured community.

The ANC's election strategy failed to expose the Group Areas Act, inferior education, limited job opportunities, inadequate housing, violence against those who opposed apartheid – in effect, the full horror and truth of the NP. And when the ANC eventually shifted its strategy, it was too late.

Politics of identification

In essence, politics is about identification. In an election, a systematic and scientific approach must be used to establish the fears, needs, aspirations and concerns of the electorate.

The ANC entered the election with three major assumptions. The first was that the coloured community would not vote for the NP because of that party's apartheid past. The second was that the United Democratic Front (UDF) had enjoyed wide support in the coloured community. This was despite a July 1992 survey by the University of the Western Cape's (UWC's) Centre for Development Studies (CDS) showing that 92 percent of coloureds had not supported the UDF.[1]

The third assumption was that leaders and public figures are decisive opinion makers. Yet no civic leaders supported the NP, no poets, no writers, no student organisations, no religious groups or movements, no trade unions, no intellectuals, no women's groups and no groups from the liberation movement. But still the NP was able to defeat the ANC and other liberation parties. How? By seeking control over the key institutions that form public opinion, the NP out-manoeuvred and out-organised its opponents.

NP election campaign

The NP's election campaign started in 1990 after Nelson Mandela's release from prison. It aimed to make the Western Cape its dominant political base. In order to do so, the NP needed to hijack political structures in the coloured community – hence its takeover of Labour Party structures.

With its experience in political marketing and electioneering, the NP set up a country-wide network, but with a keen focus on the Western Cape. By virtue of its influence and control over the main instruments of mass media communication, it was able to set the social and political agenda.

The NP used a number of forms of propaganda prior to and between 1990 and 1994 to disseminate its ideology. These included:
- propaganda of agitation, aimed at exploiting conflict;
- propaganda of integration, aimed at encouraging conformity and stabilising the social system;
- vertical propaganda, where leaders tried to influence their followers;
- horizontal propaganda, where individuals within the same group influenced their peers;

- rational propaganda, which relied on logic;
- irrational propaganda aimed at feelings and emotions.

The Strategic Committee (Stratcom), part of the National Security Management System of the apartheid regime, was a covert NP project designed to use taxpayers' money to influence the outcome of a "democratic election" in favour of the NP.

Through its network of patronage and its paid soldiers of racism, the NP was able to call on support from a number of quarters. One should not underestimate the influence the NP commanded through systematic patronage in terms of jobs, grants, contracts and perks provided to sympathisers. Given that the beneficiaries of such patronage and their families stood to lose in the event of an NP defeat, pure self interest was clearly a key motivating factor in mobilising support for the NP.

Racist-inspired violence

It is no coincidence that, in the run-up to the elections, tension between the African communities of Khayelitsha, Nyanga and Langa and the coloured communities of Mitchells Plain and Manenberg exploded periodically in the form of train violence. This pointed to the active promotion of inter-community violence, fear and suspicion prior to the election. Racism was used by the NP as a means of winning votes and mobilising against the ANC, whose majority support base is African.

Likewise, there was an orchestrated takeover by some Africans of houses allocated to coloureds in Tafelsig in Mitchells Plain. This succeeded in instilling among coloured people fears that an ANC election victory would mean they would lose their homes. *Agents provocateurs* were used to heighten these fears and in many coloured areas there were stories of Africans threatening people working in their gardens with a clear message: *"Maak mooi skoon. Wanneer Mandela president is, gaan ek die huis kry."* ("Make the place nice and clean. When Mandela is president, I am going to get this house.")

The NP also promoted a stereotype of Africans as violent people who necklaced their opponents. An official NP election magazine (which was condemned as racist by the Independent Electoral Commission) went so far as to suggest that coloureds would be necklaced by Africans. Such strategies whipped up coloured fears, with some people asking: "If Africans can do that to their own people what are they going to do to us?" The culmination of this stereotype was to link Africans, necklacing – and the ANC.

Seduced by racism

But why were so many coloured people seduced by NP propaganda and its use of racism? The comments of psychologist Julian Sonn are helpful in understanding the various forms of racism:

> White racism, or the assumption that West is best, or white is right, continues to dominate the social, economic, historical, political and psychological realities. White racism also means the use of power to institutionalise attitudes and beliefs

> ... It is helpful to distinguish between white racism and internalised white racism.
> The message that white is right has been internalised by many. The concept is
> similar to internalised oppression. (Personal letter from Sonn, 26 May 1995)

New Yorker journalist Bill Finnegan (personal letter from Finnegan, 8 June 1995) suggests a
number of reasons why the NP won the election, including:
- language and culture, since NP supporters and the coloured community are both mainly
  Afrikaans speaking;
- the Afrikaans press, which is openly anti-ANC and pro-NP;
- conservatism or fear of change, which resulted in a "better the devil you know" attitude;
- ignorance, since many uneducated voters who received pensions or disability grants believed
  they got these from the NP;
- psychological identification with the oppressor as a result of propaganda and other forms of
  social control;
- mass amnesia, as nobody seemed to want to talk about the history of forced removals, the
  Immorality Act and other discriminatory laws.

A further factor that contributed to an NP victory was the ANC's inaccurate analysis of Western Cape dynamics. The ANC failed to organise a united front incorporating all groupings opposed to the NP. It also failed to understand the fears of the coloured community and the extent to
which centuries of propaganda targetted at generations of coloureds had psychologically damaged a significant sector of that community. The ANC did not appreciate the extent of control
exercised by the social institutions responsible for opinion making, among these the education
system and the mass media, nor did it grasp the role of language and culture.

Contributing to the ANC election misfortunes was the choice of Allan Boesak as regional
leader. A July 1992 survey by Cheryl Hendricks of UWC's Centre for Development Studies
showed that coloured voters were more interested in personalities than in political parties, and
that 74,8 percent of coloured voters supported De Klerk. Accordingly, the choice of Boesak,
given the controversy surrounding his political leadership and personal life, was an ill-conceived
one.

Also of relevance to this analysis is the role of the Congress of South African Trade Unions
(Cosatu), a political ally of the ANC, which failed to seek a workers' front to unite Western Cape
unions against racism. Cosatu was approached by the Metal and Electrical Workers Union of
South Africa (Mewusa), which is affiliated to the National Council of Trade Unions (Nactu), with
a view to instituting such a campaign. Little came of this overture and it was left to Mewusa to
mobilise support for the ANC without financial or organisational support from the ANC. Nevertheless, Mewusa's intervention showed that it was possible to win support away from the NP.
Many workers did not know what the issues were; their main source of information was television
and radio; their understanding of the problems created by the NP was minimal; their sense of
history was limited. Yet Mewusa believes that, through active campaigning, it was able to swing
thousands of voters away from the NP. In a bid to achieve the somewhat more difficult outcome of
getting workers to actually vote for the ANC, Mewusa urged workers to "vote for the party that can
defeat racism and create jobs".

Conclusion

The NP can and must be defeated in the Western Cape. The liberation struggle is incomplete while the party responsible for oppression and suffering continues to occupy a position of power as the regional government of the Western Cape.

We cannot fully address national unity and end racist practices while a largely white, male-dominated party governs in this region. Our future is only certain if we can understand our past and come to terms with who we are as a community. How many suicides were caused by the Immorality Act? How many families were divided by the Group Areas Act? How many people were injured or killed because of apartheid? The Truth and Reconciliation Commission must expose, among other things, human rights abuses suffered by this community. Furthermore, the broader history of conquest, dispossession, slavery and other forms of oppression imposed on the coloured community must be understood and acknowledged. ▲

Endnote

1. The CDS research also found that 66 percent of respondents regard themselves as coloured, while 78,6 percent of Afrikaans speakers regard themselves as a distinct social group and 59 percent of English speakers hold the same view. The writer does not subscribe to the term coloured.

References

Centre for Development Studies (1992) *A study of the potential voting behaviour of persons classified coloured* (Cape Town: University of the Western Cape).

De Wet, J (1988) *The Art of Persuasive Communication* (Cape Town: Juta).

Ellul, J (1967) *The Technological Society* (New York: Random House).

Hyman, R (1975) *Industrial Relations: A Marxist Introduction* (London: MacMillan).

Chapter 5

From independence to identification [1]

Jeremy Seekings
Senior Lecturer
Sociology Department, University of Cape Town

The NP campaign constantly flirted with racism as it contrasted the new NP and its leader, FW de Klerk, with an ANC committed to Africanisation and responsible for disorder. The NP succeeded in defining the way in which the issues were understood – to its advantage and the ANC's disadvantage.

Importance of the coloured vote

Coloured voters comprise a small minority of the national electorate: only nine percent of the estimated total of 23 million eligible voters in South Africa. But in the Western Cape, they form the majority of the electorate. The estimated 1,3 to 1,4 million eligible coloured voters in this region represent between 55 and 58 percent of the regional electorate. (These figures are, of course, only estimates since neither the total adult population nor the number of people classifiable as coloured is known.) The Western Cape is unique among the major provinces in South Africa in that African voters represent a minority of the electorate.

The demographic composition of the Western Cape electorate was one reason why the major political parties – the National Party (NP) and African National Congress (ANC) – viewed winning the votes of coloured people as the top priority in their campaigns in the run-up to the April 1994 elections.

This posed a strategic dilemma for both parties: they had to try to build support among coloured voters without losing existing supporters to other parties (that is, to parties seen as championing white or African interests). In practice, both the NP and ANC concentrated their efforts on coloured voters. Their belief that few white or African supporters would defect proved correct.

The NP emerged as the victor in the contest for the support of coloured voters, thereby winning control of the region. The party won 53 percent of the total provincial vote to the ANC's 33 percent. This victory was based on the fact that the NP won about three times as many votes from coloured people as did the ANC. What, then, was the key to the NP's success?

Before addressing this question, we must clarify what we mean by "the coloured vote". Are coloured voters in some sense different or unique? One line of inquiry would lead us to the old debate around the category "coloured" and the ways in which it has been socially constructed (including by coloured people themselves). Let me leave that debate to others. A second line of inquiry concerns the empirical question of whether coloured voters actually do vote differently from other voters, that is, whether being coloured affects how or why they vote and especially how much it does so relative to other factors. In South Africa this is all too often taken for granted, reflecting the assumptions of the scholars concerned rather than the verifiable characteristics of coloured voters, their attitudes and behaviour.

I would like to take a step back and ask the same questions of coloured voters in the Western Cape that we might ask of voters anywhere else in the world. My discussion will draw primarily on two opinion polls. The first was conducted in July and August 1993, that is, eight months before the elections. It was organised by Research Initiatives. Some of the evidence used here is discussed further in a paper co-authored with Matt Eldridge (Eldridge and Seekings, 1995). The second poll, commissioned by Idasa, was conducted in August and September 1994, that is, several months after the elections. I rely here on the analysis of this poll by Robert Mattes (Mattes, 1995).

Party identification

How do voters decide which party they are going to vote for? Do they actually consider in detail the advantages and disadvantages of the rival parties' leadership and policies before coming to a decision?

For many voters in established representative democracies, including in the United States, this is often "not" the case. According to one of the leading introductory texts on voting behaviour:

> Ordinary voters do *not* think very long or very hard about political questions. Their lives are dominated by private and personal concerns – their health, their family, their friends [and, we should add in South Africa, making ends meet]. These are the things that give them most pleasure and most pain, the things that demand their most immediate attention. For most people most of the time, politics is peripheral ... Most people think about politics *some* of the time and most

people know a *little* about it. But relatively few think *very much* about politics or have *extensive* knowledge about parties, policies or personalities (Harrop and Miller, 1987: 101-2).

For many voters in North America and elsewhere, the act of voting is not so much an *instrumental* activity as an *expression* of deep-rooted allegiance to one party, an allegiance developed over years, decades or even generations. Voters can be socialised into identifying with a party through family, friends, work-mates and fellow worshippers in church. They may never seriously consider voting for an alternative party. This model of voting behaviour is generally known as the "party identification model" (Campbell et al, 1960).

Is this the case in South Africa? There is evidence indicating that it is true for large numbers of whites and Africans. Almost all white South African voters have had the privilege of participating in elections since they reached the voting age. The white party system has remained broadly stable since the early 1980s, if not longer. Over half the white electorate in the Western Cape identified clearly with one or other political party in mid-1993. Among the strongest evidence for this, ironically, is the number of white voters who identified with one party but actually voted for another in 1994. In most cases they identified with the Democratic Party or the Freedom Front but voted for the NP (Mattes, 1995: 15).

Party identification is even stronger among Africans, with a high level of allegiance to the ANC. In the Western Cape, only three percent of African voters did *not* consider themselves supporters of a political party in 1993. This high level of identification reflects on the one hand the pre-eminence of the ANC in the struggle for democracy over the past 50 years, and on the other the importance of family, friends and neighbours in shaping the political knowledge and beliefs of African voters (Mattes, 1995: 42).

The situation among coloured voters has been very different. In the Western Cape in mid-1993, less than one in four coloured voters identified with one or other political party; 76 percent did not consider themselves to be supporters of any party. This is not surprising, as none of the political parties of 1994 had campaigned for the votes of coloured people for 40-odd years. The NP had been the agent of generalised discrimination against coloured South Africans while the ANC and its unbanned allies had too often seemed to be indifferent or at least unconvincing. Whatever popular allegiance the Labour Party might have enjoyed – whether dating from its militancy in the late 1960s and early 1970s or based on its distribution of patronage in the late 1980s – this ceased to be a significant factor by 1990. Thus in 1994 coloured voters were "up for grabs" in the sense that few had a deep-rooted allegiance to any of the competing parties.

Indeed, the most important feature of the electorate in the Western Cape in 1993/94 was the high proportion of voters who were independent of the competing parties, that is, did not identify closely with any of them. A total of 51 percent of all Western Cape voters could be classified as "independent" voters in mid-1993. Four out of five of these independent voters were coloured. The weakness of coloured voters' allegiances to parties was reflected in the much higher level of support shown for individual political leaders, especially NP leader FW de Klerk, than for the parties they led. The NP recognised this in its campaign and constantly emphasised De Klerk.

The story of the elections in the Western Cape was essentially the story of the NP's success in persuading most of these independent coloured voters to vote for the NP. By mid-1993 a significant number of independent voters had already decided that they would vote for the NP, even if

Table 5.1:

The coloured vote in the Western Cape 1993/94

Party	Declared voting intention, mid-1993 %	Estimated voting behaviour, April 94 %
NP	31	57
ANC	14	20
DP	5	5
Uncommitted	50	
Did not vote		18
Total	100	100

NB: The estimates for voting in the actual elections are very rough.

they did not yet identify with it. But many more remained uncommitted. Table 5.1 presents the voting pattern among coloured voters in mid-1993.

A full 50 percent of coloured voters were uncommitted at this point. The election outcome remained uncertain, with the NP's lead over the ANC among coloured and white voters largely offset by the ANC's overwhelming support among African voters in the region.

Over the course of the election campaign in late 1993 and early 1994, the NP recruited many initially uncommitted voters. In April 1994, I estimate (very roughly) that about half of the 1993 uncommitted voters cast their vote for the NP. The reason why we have to resort to estimates is because votes in the election were not tallied according to any racial criteria, and there was a prohibition on exit polls which might have provided a reasonably accurate picture.

The NP thus built a solid support base among voters who did not initially identify with the party. The ANC, on the other hand, failed to extend its support base much beyond its initial core of highly committed supporters. (Almost all of the voters who declared in mid-1993 that they would vote for the ANC also identified closely with that party; in the case of the NP, by contrast, almost two out of three of its declared voters were independents). Mattes has drawn on Idasa's post-election polling research to suggest that many coloured voters have now come to identify with the NP, that is, they consider themselves supporters of the NP beyond just voting for it (Mattes, 1995: 13). But the scope and resilience of this identification remains unclear.

What explains the NP's success in recruiting uncommitted voters to the NP and turning some independents into NP identifiers? Many commentators have treated this as the obvious result of coloured voters' racial or cultural allegiances. Coloured voters, it is suggested, would obviously vote with white voters; alternatively, Afrikaans-speaking, Dutch Reformed Church-going (DRC) coloured voters would obviously vote with Afrikaans-speaking, DRC-going white voters. This is not so self-evident to me. For one thing, as late as mid-1993, the NP could only count on the support of one in three coloured voters in this region, and probably ended up with the votes of little more than one in two (that is, taking uncommitted voters and non-voters into account). For another, the NP also won many votes from Indian South Africans in KwaZulu-Natal, although Indians are neither DRC-going nor Afrikaans-speaking, as Heribert Adam has pointed out (Adam, 1994).

Coloured voters have certainly not been socialised over the years or decades into supporting the NP. All in all, it seems to me that we need a more detailed explanation of *why* so many (but far from all) coloured voters *swung* behind the NP. We should not take the outcome for granted.

Issue voting

The party-identification model provides one approach to understanding voter behaviour. The other major model focuses on issues. Issue voting can be retrospective, in that voters assess the rival parties' past performance on the issues that the voters consider most important. Alternatively, it can be forward-looking in that voters assess the parties' election programmes. Of course, these two strands can be combined (and they can in turn be woven together with elements of the party-identification model).

The major parties certainly campaigned as if issues were all-important, and each major party claimed to espouse non-racialism. The issue focus was clearest in the case of the ANC, which based its campaign around its Reconstruction and Development Programme (RDP), or "Our Plan" as the party called it. As the ANC's United States adviser, Stan Greenberg, put it: "You have an electorate that's serious; South Africans are not just voting to affirm history; they're voting for a direction and a set of policies" (Eldridge and Seekings, 1995). The RDP was supposed to set out the ANC's direction and policies with regard to education, housing, job creation and so on.

What did coloured voters consider to be the most important issues in the election? In polls, they consistently identified the issues of unemployment (or the economy) and political violence. Table 5.2 presents the responses to a question asked in the mid-1993 poll. Coloured voters identified the same factors – together with crime – when asked: "What are the things going wrong in this country?" (When asked what was going right, most said "nothing"!) The same general pattern was found in Idasa's post-election survey (see Table 5.3, although this data is for coloured voters nation-wide, not just in the Western Cape).

These issues – violence and employment/the economy – were identified as the most important problems by African, Indian and white voters as well as coloured voters in the country as a whole. This was true both before the election, in mid-1993, and at the time of the election, according to responses in Idasa's post-election poll.

These issues were also identified by ANC voters, NP voters and uncommitted voters. There is no neat correlation between party preference and issue chosen (although NP supporters in the

Table 5.2:

Issues in the election (1993)

What is the most important problem that a new government should work on after the election? (Coloured voters, Western Cape, mid-1993)

	NP voters %	ANC voters %	uncommitted voters %	all voters %
Unemployment/ the economy	33	38	27	31
Political violence	31	20	29	26
Racial discrimination/ apartheid	6	9	2	5
Housing	4	8	5	5
Education	4	4	3	3
Don't know	5	3	15	11

country as a whole attach marginally more importance to crime and violence, and ANC supporters country-wide to jobs). But what do voters understand by these issues? It is possible that voters view these issues differently, leading some to blame the NP and others the ANC.

Probing beneath the statistics

Let us consider first the issue of jobs and the economy. Whom did coloured voters hold responsible, and whom did they think would deal best with the issue? In the mid-1993 poll, prospective coloured voters were asked if they agreed with a series of statements about the NP and ANC. Responses to two statements about the economy are presented in Table 5.4.

Most ANC voters blamed the NP, while NP voters were sure that an ANC government would make the problem worse. Uncommitted voters were somewhat ambivalent but tended to favour the ANC less than the NP.

So why did coloured voters view the issue of unemployment differently and respond to it differently? One part of the answer concerns the views of these voters in general. In other words, a voter's views on unemployment were often bound up with views on the state of the country and on social and economic transformation.

Across the country, voters who were optimistic about changes were the people who declared their expectation by voting for the ANC. Voters who were gloomy were NP voters. In racial terms, white voters were particularly gloomy, African voters most upbeat and coloured voters torn be-

Table 5.3:

Issues in the 1994 (post-election poll)

What was the most important problem at the time of the election?
(Coloured voters, nationally, Idasa post-election survey)

	all voters %
Unemployment/ the economy	36
Political violence	41
Racial discrimination/ apartheid	10
Housing	8
Education	5

tween optimism and pessimism. Most voters also clearly identified the ANC as a left-wing or radical party, and the NP as right wing or conservative (Mattes and Gouws, 1995: 31-7).

This could be interpreted in either racial or class terms. Whites may be gloomy about losing out because they are white, or because egalitarian socio-economic change will erode their privileges. The position of coloured voters provides something of a test case. Among coloured voters there were both pessimists (mostly NP or uncommitted voters) and optimists (mostly ANC voters). Is there any non-racial basis for explaining why some coloured voters were optimistic and ANC-inclined while others were pessimistic and NP-inclined?

Among coloured voters in the Western Cape there is a clear correlation between socio-economic class or educational attainment, on the one hand, and optimism about change and voting intention, on the other. ANC support is drawn predominantly from better educated coloured voters, and especially from the "new middle class" of teachers, civil servants and private sector bureaucrats (Mattes, 1995: 25). NP support is drawn disproportionately from the coloured working class. Table 5.5 presents a breakdown of Western Cape voters by race and education (which can be loosely regarded as a proxy for class).

The class structure of support among coloured voters for both the ANC and NP differs sharply from the class structure of their respective support bases among African and white voters.

The correlation between class and voting intention among coloured voters may reflect different socialisation patterns. The teaching profession, for example, has long been a stronghold of radical thought in coloured areas. It is possible that radical tendencies are passed on from generation to generation, and are reinforced through the more politicised high schools and teacher training colleges. Further research into the political orientations of different members (and generations) of families would shed light on this.

Table 5.4:

Percentage of coloured Western Cape voters who agree "a lot" or "a little" with statements on the economy (mid-1993)

	NP voters %	ANC voters %	uncommitted voters %	all voters %
"The NP has ruined our economy and created unemployment"	21	83	25	31
"An ANC government will mismanage the economy"	70	12	36	43

The more likely explanation surely concerns the confidence that voters have about transferring their assets and skills into the new South Africa. ANC support is concentrated among the new middle class because these voters have skills which can be marketed in the new as much as the old South Africa, and because their access to resources such as housing depends more on their financial clout in impersonal markets than on political patronage. Working-class coloured voters, by contrast, are threatened by the removal of the privilege of state patronage and protection in the labour and housing markets (Cameron, 1989; Giliomee, 1994: 51-2). The skills and assets of working-class coloured voters are not readily transferable into the new South Africa, and they face far more serious competition from African workers and homeless people. Most importantly, perhaps, working-class coloured voters see their prospects threatened by affirmative action aimed at the advancement of Africans (this is repeatedly stressed in focus group discussions). For working-class coloured voters, the employment issue is primarily about ensuring equal opportunity for jobs.

The ANC's election campaign did not address these fears effectively. Coloured voters might have been convinced that the ANC had an impressive "Plan" to build houses and provide jobs, but they seem to have remained sceptical that they themselves would benefit. Polls repeatedly showed widespread wariness of the ANC among coloured voters – especially among the less educated and working class. This wariness is shown in Table 5.6.

The NP campaign, on the other hand, was effective in linking voters' fears to the spectre of a destructive ANC. When African squatters occupied houses built for coloured families, the NP warned (coloured) voters that their houses were "not safe under the ANC". Its newspaper advertising proclaimed: "The ANC is not yet part of the government and already its supporters are taking houses which belong to legitimate owners." A widely used slogan was: "Stop the comrades, vote NP." Fears or negative perceptions of the ANC were probably more important than positive perceptions of the NP. The campaign of the latter constantly flirted with racism as it contrasted the new NP and its leader, De Klerk, with an ANC committed to Africanisation and responsible for disorder. The NP succeeded in defining the way in which the issues were under-

Table 5.5

Voting intentions by race and class, mid-1993

	White	Coloured	African	% of electorate
post-matric	□□□□□□ ▲▲▲▲▲ ■■	▲▲▲ ■	■	18
std 9-10	□□□ ▲▲▲	□□□□ ▲▲ ■■■	■■■	18
std 5-8	□□□ ▲▲▲	□□□□□□□□□ ▲▲▲▲▲▲▲▲ ▲▲▲▲▲▲▲ ■■	■■■■■ ■■■■■	43
std 4 or less		□□□□ ▲▲▲▲▲▲▲▲ ■	■■■■■	19

Each symbol represents 1% of the total Western Cape electorate.
NP support is marked by □
ANC support is marked by ■
A ▲ indicates either 'uncommitted' voters or voters supporting a minor party.

stood – to its advantage and the ANC's disadvantage (Giliomee, 1994; Eldridge and Seekings, 1995).

As is clear from this final section, the quantitative evidence from survey research is useful for identifying correlations between variables (as well as revealing the absence of correlations). But it is less useful in terms of interpretation. Survey-based research needs to be combined with qualitative research, including focus groups and detailed individual interviews.

Prospects

Let me briefly summarise my argument. Few coloured voters in the Western Cape identified with any political party as late as mid-1993. During 1993/94 substantial numbers of independent

Table 5.6:

Perceptions of the ANC and NP
(coloured Western Cape voters, 1993)

	NP voters %	ANC voters %	uncommitted voters %	all voters %
Agree "a lot" or "a little"' "An ANC government will neglect the problems of coloureds, Indians and whites"	74	13	40	46
"Which party or parties has a place for people like [the respondent]?"				
NP	84	5	25	37
ANC	7	85	14	19

coloured voters were recruited to vote for the NP which consequently won the election. In the course of this, many of these initially independent voters came to identify with the NP. The NP's support was strongest among working-class coloured voters, whose fears of socio-economic and political transformation were played upon by the NP's campaign messages.

Coloured voters in South Africa during the current transition are not unlike many voters in the former Communist Party-ruled countries of central and eastern Europe (Evans and Whitefield, 1993). Socio-economic and political changes involve winners and losers as well as considerable uncertainty. That South Africans' perceptions of such changes are fragmented along racial as well as class lines reflects the ways in which class formation was deeply shaped and dependent on the racially discriminatory policies of the apartheid state.

But just as the legacy of apartheid will not disappear overnight, nor are current voting patterns set in stone. How committed are coloured voters to the NP? Did 1994 represent a period of lasting realignment or an episode that will be shown to have run against the long-term trend? Are the key issues likely to change? Some data suggests strong party identification by late 1994 (Mattes, 1995: 13). But to answer this question adequately, we need much more detailed information about patterns of political socialisation – voters' allegiance to the NP is presumably yet to be reinforced through the networks of family life, friends, associations and so on – and on processes of class formation and voters' perceptions of their social and economic interests in the new South Africa. ▲

Endnote

1. This paper draws on research conducted with Matt Eldridge, a postgraduate student at the University of Cape Town, and on work in progress with Bob Mattes of Idasa's Public Information Centre.

References

Adam, H (1994) "Ethnic versus civic nationalism: South Africa's non-racialism in comparative perspective", in *South African Sociological Review*, Vol 7, No 1.

Campbell, A, P Converse, WE Miller and DE Stokes (1960) *The American Voter* (New York: Wiley).

Cameron, R (1989) "An analysis of the 1988 coloured municipal elections in the Western Cape", unpublished paper, University of Cape Town.

Eldridge, M and J Seekings (1995) "An uphill battle: Voter attitudes and ANC strategy in the Western Cape in the 1994 South African elections", unpublished paper, University of Cape Town.

Evans, G and S Whitefield (1993) "Identifying the bases of party competition in eastern Europe", in *British Journal of Political Science*, No 23.

Giliomee, H (1994) "The National Party's campaign for a liberation election", in A Reynolds (ed), *Election '94 South Africa: The Campaigns, Results and Future Prospects* (Cape Town: David Philip).

Harrop, M and W Miller (1987) *Elections and Voters: A Comparative Introduction* (London: Macmillan).

Mattes, R (1995) "The limited impact of race and ethnicity on partisan identification in South Africa's first open election", unpublished paper.

Mattes, R and A Gouws (1995) "Race, ethnicity and voting behaviour: Lessons from South Africa", unpublished paper.

Chapter 6

The devil who keeps promises

Wilmot James
Executive Director
Institute for Democracy in South Africa

When FW de Klerk promised in 1990 that he and his party would remove racial classification, group areas, open up the political process and make a deal with the organisations of the black majority, he kept his word on every item.

In the national elections of April 1994, the coloured community gave 68 percent of its votes to the National Party (NP), 25 percent to the African National Congress (ANC), five percent to the Democratic Party, and less than one percent each to the Pan Africanist Congress of Azania and Inkatha Freedom Party.

As 61 percent of the coloured vote is concentrated in the Western Cape, it was because of this coloured support that the region became the only province where the NP dominated, giving it the NP's Hernus Kriel as premier and four NP Members of the Executive Committee in a six-strong legislature of national unity. Over half (52 percent) of the NP's support came from the coloured community, with the bulk of the balance of support coming from white constituencies.

How does one read the election outcome? One is tempted to pause at the irony of the results. The NP was the architect of apartheid and a hard-nosed champion of white sectional interests. Not that long ago the same black people who voted for the NP were harassed and persecuted by race laws and colour bars, were subjected to paternalistic and exploitative treatment by the public service and police, and were hustled in and out of their homes under Group Areas legislation as if they were so many pieces of filth.

In the dying decade of apartheid, activists drawn from coloured communities, mainly younger people, participated in the progressive structures of the day to dismantle apartheid. As a result, they were treated with a severity of political repression at least equal to that handed down to other political opponents of the system. The irony is that this historical memory did not translate into widespread votes for the ANC, the dominant party of liberation; it was the erstwhile party of oppression that drew votes.

ANC's lack of credibility

Let it be said that in party political terms the choices available were confusing, culturally dense and complicated. On the one hand, the ANC was familiar to only a relatively small section of coloured leadership; it did not penetrate very deeply into the soul of the people. The dismantling of the United Democratic Front, and the manner in which this was done, seemed to confirm suspicions of an imminent disregard on the part of the ANC for those things coloured activists looked upon as important.

The ANC was largely seen as the face of black African majoritarianism. It is true that prejudice, racism and historical ignorance strongly influenced the reception of the ANC in certain circles. People did not know about or understand the concept of non-racialism; but more importantly, they had little faith in the notion and saw it as deception. Even Nelson Mandela's many gestures could not dispel the feeling that the ANC's non-racialism was dressed-up Xhosa ethno-nationalism waiting to unleash itself.

The strategy of presenting Allan Boesak, and later Archie Vergotini and Franklin Sonn, as the face of the ANC in the Western Cape failed to promote much trust in the credibility of the organisation. At the time of the election, Boesak was a victim of the tendency to read the political credibility of a person from his or her personal credibility, where the latter was judged harshly against conservative notions of marital fidelity and life-long loyalty to one's spouse.

Vergotini was unknown outside of certain teacher circles while Sonn was seen as lacking in consistent political conviction. In coloured communities, one is not easily allowed to change political stance. Certainly, in Unity Movement circles, changing one's mind to adapt to a shifting political environment is regarded as evidence of opportunism, of blowing with the wind, of a deficiency in core political values.

The NP, on the other hand, was seen to have finally arrived at its senses. Here was a party which had systematically and brutally prised away a people from their larger kin in culture and language on the basis of colour and appearance – and putative lines of descent when that did not work.

Now the NP was asking the sons and daughters, the grandsons and granddaughters of the excluded to join them in their quest to protect the rights of all minorities, defined in cultural rather than racial terms, against a threatening black majority. The *boere*, the *baas*, had finally been brought down from his arrogant pedestal to ask the *kleurlinge* for help. It was a moment some people had been waiting for. What historical triumph!

Though they would strenuously deny it, some people derived psychic delight, under the framework of the liberation struggle, from getting the *boere* to bow and scrape, to apologise, to publicly acknowledge how rotten they had been to a part of their family.

NP's credibility of intent

The appeal of the NP in some (largely working-class) quarters was the credibility of its purpose and intent. This raises an issue of faith and trust in the political process. In the past, when the NP said it would oppress, exploit, engineer in the mad vision of racialism, it delivered on these threats. When the Group Areas Act was passed, coloured leaders widely proclaimed on the impossibility of such a mission. Sadly, they were proved wrong in that over 300 000 coloureds had been forcibly removed by 1976.

At issue is the importance of keeping one's promise, of the peculiar morality of the institution of promises, even when that promise comes at one's own expense. When FW de Klerk promised in 1990 that he and his party would remove racial classification, group areas, open up the political process and make a deal with the organisations of the black majority, he kept his word on every item.

The devil who kept his promise became an angel who did likewise. Opinion polls showed De Klerk to be the favoured leader by far in the coloured community before the 1994 elections.

Another interesting point is that the NP did not make the mistake of using the designation "so-called" in addressing coloured people. Why this was the case is unclear: was it because the party at last understood the humiliation of outsider definition, coming as it did from a community which prided itself to a fault on assertive self-identification? Or was it because the NP received good advice from its black brethren?

Perhaps it was none of these things but rather sheer laziness, habit, unwillingness to take on the choreography of scratching the air. Perhaps it is because there is no good Afrikaans translation of "so-called". Whatever the reason, rather than referring to coloured people as "so-called", NP leaders preferred *bruin mense* or, in rural areas, *kleurlinge*. Also, NP leaders communicated with obvious ease in Afrikaans whereas when the ANC tried, it sounded laboured and was thus received as insincere, almost patronising.

The meaning of "so-called" is odd and contradictory because it all depends on who says it. When a person uses it in reference to himself or herself, the term is acceptable: it is often viewed as the most progressive way of aligning yourself, of placing a clear distance between you and those outsiders who dare to label you as coloured. But for the very same reason, when a white person calls coloured people "so-called" coloured people or, even worse, when a black African person does so, the suspicion is that what they really mean is *Hotnot* (Hottentot) or *Boesman* (Bushman).[1]

It is not an unusual phenomenon: when African-Americans refer to themselves, among themselves, as "niggers", it is received in jest with no hostile intent presumed. If you listen to actor Richard Pryor, it is even funny. If a white American dared try the same thing, all hell would break loose. The meaning behind "so-called" depends vitally on who says it, whether that person is *of* the group or *outside* the group. I recently witnessed an audience bristle when a black African panellist referred to coloured people as "so-called" coloureds.

On a political level, the NP offered to protect the rights of minorities (coloured people were included in the NP's discourse on cultural and language minorities) and outlined a limited perspective on change. By contrast, the ANC promised and threatened radical change. The NP spoke about the liberalisation of the economy; the ANC spoke about socialism (that has changed). The NP wanted strong regional and provincial powers; the ANC wanted to turn provincial govern- ments into the administrative arms of central government (that has not changed).

The NP could not defend the special intermediate protection of coloured people in the former racial order (in particular, special labour markets), but replaced coloured labour preference with the protection of minority interests. The ANC had no such protection device, illusory as it might be. The NP did not talk about affirmative action; the ANC insisted on its importance.

In sum, the NP offered the liberalisation of economy and state, the primacy of individual rights and the defence of culturally-based minority interests; the ANC promised transformation of economy and state, non-racialism and corrective justice for the previously disadvantaged. It is not surprising that the coloured vote tended to follow class lines. The least vulnerable to radical change, the middle classes, tended to vote ANC. The most vulnerable to affirmative action labour market pressures, the working classes, went with the NP.

Role of racism

There are those who say that coloured people did not vote for the ANC because they have racist attitudes towards Africans, and that the same people voted for the NP because of their racist affinity to whites. More worrying is the perception that, in the aftermath of the election, some coloureds reject black Africans but accept whites for racist reasons.

This line of reasoning is problematic. Firstly, there is no evidence to support the claim that coloured people are any more racist than anyone else. In the absence of such evidence, I assume that coloured people are no more and no less racist than any other South African. This is by no means an excuse or justification of racism among coloured people or anyone else – including, it should be noted, black African people – but it is to say that to interpret the coloured vote as an act of racism has little basis in fact.

Secondly, public opinion results suggest that coloured people voted for those parties seen to be most capable of responding to some real problems and concerns in their respective communi- ties. Whether the perception of party competence was misplaced is not the issue. What is at issue is that coloured people at the time of the elections felt that violence and crime, unemployment and poverty were their most pressing concerns, and that they distributed their vote in part to those parties perceived as capable of addressing these issues.

A second worrying tendency is the portrayal of coloured people who voted for the NP (or more accurately, who did not vote for the ANC) as "traitors". Some very senior political figures have made this unfortunate claim, unfortunate because a traitor is someone disloyal to the state. "Treach- ery" is to sell-out, to betray, to subvert the core values of the state. The jurisprudential equivalent of "treachery" is sedition. In authoritarian orders, as in the previous apartheid one, "treachery" had the legal equivalent of "terrorism" or "communism".

It is perverse to argue that voting for a legitimate party, however despicable its history, is an act of "treason". Though far more time has lapsed in the United States, no one would argue that voting for the Democrats is "treachery" because the Democratic Party supported slavery in the 19th century. One should be careful not to confuse party with state, loyalty to a party with loyalty to the state. The ANC might govern, but it is not the state. It is undemocratic to suggest, by using the term "traitors", that voting for the ANC is reducible to loyalty and patriotism to the state.

It is particularly upsetting when considering some survey material on coloured loyalty and solidarity patterns. In one survey, asked whether they considered themselves part of a distinctive community, 47 percent of coloured respondents said they did (in contrast to 61 percent of black Africans and 82 percent of whites). More importantly, of all groups surveyed, the coloured respondents identified themselves most strongly as South African first, coloured second.

Other material convincingly demonstrates a strong loyalty among coloured people to being South African, and an allegiance to the state and its democratic institutions reconfigured as they were after the 1994 elections. Key leaders from the coloured community are in government to live out their commitment and loyalty to democratic state institutions.

There is no evidence of treachery here, no commitment to sedition, and even the most recently formed fringe separatist groups consider the state to be unfair, lacking in even-handedness, but not illegitimate.

There is no single, anthropologically homogeneous, coloured community. There are many communities, bound together by decades of exclusion and a rootlessness created by group areas. There are Malays and Christians; Afrikaans speakers, English speakers and masters of the Cape Flats patois; people of Cape Town and people of the Boland, of Outeniqua, Griqualand and Gauteng. This is a diverse group of folks who, like South Africa itself, belong to this soil and this history but are finding it difficult to come home, to finally feel that they belong.

Endnote

1. *Hotnot* and *Boesman* are both used as derogatory references to coloured people.

References

Independent Electoral Commission (April 1994) Provincial Count (Electoral Administration Department: Western Cape).

Institute for Multi-Party Democracy (February 1994) *"Launching Democracy: Sixth Report"* (Cape Town: Institute for Multi-Party Democracy).

Reynolds, A (ed) *Election '94 South Africa* (Cape Town: David Philip).

Table 6.1:

Distribution of the coloured vote

	Votes Cast (Coloured)	%	Votes Cast (Province)	%
Western Cape	1 175 758	61,0	2 137 742	55,0
Eastern Cape	218 167	11,3	2 908 906	7,5
Northern Cape	205 923	10,7	403 772	51,0
Gauteng	167 930	8,7	4 198 250	4,0
KwaZulu-Natal	58 629	3,0	3 664 324	1,6
North West	47 164	2,4	1 572 142	3,0
Orange Free State	40 628	2,1	1 354 266	3,0
Eastern Transvaal	13 260	0,7	1 326 068	1,0
North Transvaal	3 840	0,2	1 920 260	0,3
TOTAL	1 931 299	100	19 485 730	10,0

Table 6.2

Votes distributed by major party – National

Community	NP	%	ANC	%
African	0,5m	03	11,50m	81
White	1,9m	66	0,05m	2
Coloured	1,2m	67	0,50m	27
Indian	0,3m	50	0,15m	25
TOTAL	3,9m	20	12,2m	62,4

Table 6.3

Coloured support for parties (Western Cape)

National Party	68,7%	807 746•
African National Congress	24,6%	289 236
Democratic Party	5,3%	62 315
Pan Africanist Congress	0,3%	3 527
Inkatha Freedom Party	0,2%	2 351
TOTAL	100	1 165 175

• estimate

Sources:

Institute for Multi-Party Democracy, "Launching Democracy: Sixth Report"; Second Western
    Cape Survey on issues relevant to a free and fair election, February 1994, p11.
Reynolds, A (ed) *Election '94 South Africa*, p191, 204.
Independent Electoral Commission, Provincial Count: April 1994.

Chapter 7

Minorities together and apart

Yunus Carrim
Member of Parliament
African National Congress

Coloureds and Indians should not be mollycoddled. They are not blind or helpless victims of a "minority syndrome". They have contributed to their alienation from the transition and must take responsibility for their choices. They are challenged to work towards a society that reconciles their needs and interests with those of Africans and other people in this country.

Subordinate minorities

As with coloureds, Indians voted overwhelmingly for the National Party (NP) in the April 1994 elections. The figures, too, are similar. It is estimated that over 60 percent of Indians voted for the NP and about 25 percent for the African National Congress (ANC), while over 65 percent of coloureds voted for the NP and over 25 percent for the ANC.[1] This article considers the voting behaviour of Indians and their attitudes towards the transition to see what parallels exist with coloureds.

Indians and coloureds are often lumped together with whites as "minorities". While this is correct in a general sense, it is not necessarily completely accurate. Given whites' economic, political and numerical weight under apartheid, they are best understood as a dominant minority whereas Indians and coloureds are subordinate minorities. This distinction is helpful in understanding the voting behaviour of Indians and coloureds and their attitudes towards the transition.

Indians constitute 2,6 percent of the population and 3 percent of the electorate [2], with 78 percent living in KwaZulu-Natal where they constitute 13 percent of the electorate.

They are by no means a monolithic group; in fact differences in terms of religion, language, customs, ancestry, political beliefs and class make this the most heterogeneous of South Africa's four racial groups. The main dividing line is religion: Hindus constitute 62 percent, Muslims 19 percent and Christians 13 percent of Indian South Africans. In general, relations between these religious groups are not conflictual, even if the groups are somewhat aloof from each other.

Caste is not significant among Hindus in South Africa. Language differences, particularly where they coincide with religious divisions, are more significant. Tamil is the major language, followed by Hindi, Gujerati, Urdu and Telegu. The 1991 census also reveals substantial income inequalities within the Indian community.

Despite this internal differentiation, Indians do, in the context of the South African population as a whole, constitute an identifiable group – and in this broad sense they constitute a homogeneous community. To understand the sense in which Indians constitute a "community", it is necessary to come to terms with the nature of both their heterogeneity and homogeneity and that this changes with varied circumstances. Identity is largely socially constructed and not immutable. At present, Indians are best understood as a racial group distinguished by physical criteria, comprising several ethnic groups distinguished by cultural criteria, including religion, language and customs.

Voting behaviour and attitudes towards the transition

As with other blacks, Indians have a long tradition of struggle against white minority rule, especially since the formation by Mahatma Gandhi of the Natal Indian Congress (NIC) in 1894.

After initially waging struggles largely on their own and around their particular needs and interests, Indians made common cause with other communities under the banner of the ANC in the 1950s and consistently rejected co-option by the white minority. In the 1980s, Indians and coloureds overwhelmingly rejected the offer of separate, subordinate chambers of a white-dominated tricameral parliament that excluded Africans.

Ultimately, given the history of Indian people, their political struggles, their subordinate position under white minority rule, the virulent anti-Indianism of the NP in the past and the prominence of Indians in the leadership of the ANC, Indians were expected to vote mainly for the ANC. Yet they voted mainly for the NP and, in the provincial elections, gave Amichand Rajbansi's Minority Front (MF) 48 951 votes to secure his seat in the KwaZulu-Natal legislature. How does one explain their voting behaviour? The explanations are complex and intricate, and will be dealt with here in a condensed form.

The state deliberately divided Indians and coloureds from Africans and, from the late 1960s, began to offer them significantly better resources and services than Africans. With these material divisions went the ideological conditioning that ensured many Indians and coloureds looked down on Africans and also saw them as a threat.

Furthermore, many issues around which Indians had historically mobilised had to some degree been met by the NP government in the 10 years or so before the April 1994 elections. Although most of the demands would not have been met had it not been for mass pressure from below, the NP was able to take credit for meeting them.

Sections of the Indian community were opposed to white minority domination because it affected them directly. But this was not accompanied by a commitment to a full non-racial democracy. The limited opposition to apartheid by some sections of the Indian community was incorrectly perceived as support for the national liberation movement.

Ultimately, the "minority psychosis" of Indians prevailed. Many Indians felt caught between the privileges and dominance of the white minority and the poverty and frustration of the African majority. The NP successfully preyed on the anxieties of Indians about a majority-rule, non-racial democracy. This was made easier by the paranoia that prevailed before the elections, with the occupation by African shackdwellers of houses allocated for Indians, escalating crime and violence and the stockpiling of food in fear that the country was going to come to a standstill. The conservatism of Indians in KwaZulu-Natal is also partly a response to the ethnic chauvinism of the Inkatha Freedom Party (IFP).

Many Indians could not accept that the ANC's affirmative action policies would also benefit them. In KwaZulu-Natal, they felt they would have to bear the brunt of affirmative action. In terms of the racial hierarchy with whites at the top, Indians and coloureds in the middle and Africans at the bottom, African advancement comes into direct conflict with the comparatively privileged position of Indians. For example, the African worker seeking promotion comes into conflict with the more established Indian, not white, worker and the emerging African trader seeking to expand has a rival in the established Indian, not white, trader.

Many Indians also reflected the prejudices of their social conditioning under apartheid. They could not accept that African people could govern the country effectively and without corruption. The persistent, violent clashes between the ANC and the IFP reinforced this feeling.

In addition, relations between Indians and Africans in KwaZulu-Natal have not been easy. There is mutual suspicion and each group harbours racial prejudices against the other. The scars of the 1949 Cato Manor and the 1985 Inanda clashes between Indians and Africans remain. The expulsion of Asians from East Africa also has a certain resonance. Many Indian South Africans feared that Africans would turn against them and therefore voted for the NP in the hope that it would be able to protect them against this.

The NP's policies on key issues preoccupying major sections of the Indian community were also much clearer and more appealing – particularly on the protection of property, language, cultural and religious rights.

Despite many of the above observations, it was not inevitable that Indians would vote mainly for the NP. In surveys conducted before the elections, it emerged that many Indians did not have strong party identification and consequently could be swung to any of the major parties. The ANC must therefore also accept responsibility for its failure to win the majority of Indian votes. Its election campaign suffered many organisational and strategic weaknesses. Space constraints do not allow for a proper consideration of this here. Ultimately, however, the three regional structures of the ANC in KwaZulu-Natal were not able to come together in an effective provincial campaign.

Key elites in the Indian community – leaders of cultural, religious, professional, welfare, sports and other organisations – came out openly in support of the ANC and endorsed it in advertisements. However, they were not able to carry their constituencies with them.

While the process of drawing up the ANC's lists of nominees for parliament was in many ways commendable, it had its weaknesses. Indians were under-represented in the list for the KwaZulu-Natal legislature: three out of 40 in the first half of the list. On the other hand, Indians were rather over-represented in the lists for the National Assembly. Several Indians who were high on the national lists were chosen because of their contribution to the national liberation movement as a whole and for their specific skills, but they did not have significant constituencies in the Indian community. Others with strong grassroots profiles in the Indian community were not prominent in the candidates' lists. Surveys before the elections consistently established that FW de Klerk was more popular with Indians than Nelson Mandela, and that De Klerk was more popular than his party. Exactly why De Klerk should have this support is difficult to tell, especially in view of the moral stature and international reputation of Mandela.

All analyses of the election results confirm that the ANC drew its support largely from the Indian middle class, while working-class Indians voted substantially for the NP. In a sense, this is understandable as Indian workers felt more vulnerable to affirmative action and other aspects of the transition than the middle class did. Interestingly, a higher proportion of Indians seem to have voted for the ANC in Gauteng. In Lenasia, which has the largest concentration of Indians in Gauteng, it is suggested that up to 70 percent voted ANC.[3] The vast majority of Indians in Lenasia are from the middle class.

At present Indians are out on a limb. They voted for the NP but it can offer them little. The IFP is in power in KwaZulu-Natal and the ANC nationally. None of the major parties touches the Indian people sufficiently and this community seems to feel alienated from the transition. This is reinforced by the effects that crime, violence, difficult economic conditions, deteriorating social services, affirmative action and the informal settlements have had on their lives since the elections. In these circumstances, Rajbansi has increasingly presented his MF as the only party that cares about the needs and interests of Indians.

On the other hand, Indians' worst fears about the transition have not been realised. It has been a remarkably moderate transition and Mandela has been outstanding in his commitment to reconciliation and nation building. His popularity has grown among Indians and the other minorities. Recent surveys have consistently showed that support for the ANC among Indians has grown.

Sociologist Kogila Moodley describes Indians as a "wavering minority".[4] Their support for the NP is far from certain. Now that the NP has shown itself to have limited power, Indians may well be susceptible to supporting other parties. For the ANC, the challenge is to respond to the needs and interests of Indian and other minorities in a way that is consistent with the needs and interests of the African majority.

Parallels with the coloured community

Much of the voting behaviour of Indians and their attitudes to the transition also applies to coloureds. These similarities expose the inadequacies of the argument that coloureds voted for the NP simply because of affinities of language, culture and blood.

As with Indians, the ANC drew its support mainly from the coloured middle class while the working class voted substantially for the NP. Also, coloured voters in areas outside the Western Cape voted in higher proportions for the ANC. In Kimberley, the majority voted for the ANC and in the Northern Cape province as a whole at least 40 percent voted ANC. In Gauteng, Schlemmer (1994: 21) estimates coloureds favoured the ANC in a ratio of roughly 5:4.

In order to understand coloureds' voting behaviour and attitudes towards the transition, it is necessary to come to terms with the sense in which coloureds constitute a "community". That "coloureds" exist at all or that they constitute a "community" is rejected with contempt by some. For those who acknowledge the existence of coloureds, even as a "social construct", it is necessary to define whether coloureds constitute a racial or ethnic group. Alternatively, are they a racial group comprising ethnic groups along lines of religion, language and ancestry? Or how else are they to be defined?

Despite many similarities in the position of Indians and coloureds, these two communities do not find each other easily. In KwaZulu-Natal, while social interaction and inter-racial marriages are on the increase, the two communities view each other with a certain disdain.

If there are similarities in the position of coloureds and Indians, there are also significant differences. The minority status of coloureds is somewhat obfuscated by the fact that they constitute a majority in the Western Cape and that no political party can come to power in the province without them. In contrast, while Indians constitute a significant 13 percent of the KwaZulu-Natal electorate – a significance accentuated by the intense IFP-ANC rivalry for support – their specific needs cannot determine the agenda in the province.

While there are racial tensions between coloureds and Africans, coloureds do not have the experience of the 1949 and 1985 confrontations between Indians and Africans. Some coloureds are descendants of the Khoi-San (even if some want to deny the association), and as such they have a claim to being indigenous. Indians, however, cannot make such a claim. Unlike Indians, coloureds also have blood ties with both Africans and whites, and there are overlaps of religion and language with Afrikaners that Indians do not share.

Despite the differences, Indians and coloureds are broadly similar in terms of voting behaviour and attitudes towards the transition. In spite of their majority status in the Western Cape, coloureds also feel alienated from the transition and this provides fertile grounds for the growth of the coloured "nationalist" movements that are emerging.

But coloureds and Indians should not be mollycoddled. They are not blind or helpless victims of a "minority syndrome". They have contributed to their alienation from the transition and must take responsibility for their choices. They are challenged to work towards a society that reconciles their needs and interests with those of Africans and other people in this country.

Coloureds and Indians fear that Africans are being allocated a disproportionately high share of the resources in the new society. It is this conflict over resources that creates the greatest potential for racial tensions. But there are historical imbalances that simply have to be redressed. It is also in the interests of coloureds and Indians that the living standards of Africans improve. The potential for conflict may well increase if Africans find that post-apartheid society is not delivering on their basic needs while coloureds and Indians continue to enjoy a relatively privileged position. Ultimately, this is not a question about race but about need. The rich of whatever colour will have to contribute to the upkeep of the poor, regardless of colour.

Reconciling multiple needs and identities

The anxieties raised by coloureds and Indians about the transition and identity have more general significance for our country. There are other groups – and yet others might surface – with similar concerns. The challenge is to respond to their needs in a way that can be reconciled with forging a non-racial, more egalitarian democracy.

The marked identities of our diverse people will not disappear overnight. The nation-building process has to be sensitive to this. People have multiple identities. It is perfectly possible, for example, for a person to be a Hindu, Indian, black and South African. The challenge before the new South Africa is to provide people with the space to express their identities in a way that fosters the evolution of a broader South African national identity. It must be possible for people to be simultaneously part of a minority and part of the whole – as part of the long-term goal of being simply South African. ▲

Endnotes

1. A precise racial breakdown of votes cast is not possible. These figures and others about the elections are drawn from A Reynolds's, *Elections '94 South Africa*; Schlemmer's, "Birth of Democracy", in *Indicator*; and internal ANC evaluations.

2. Figures on the social structure and composition of the Indian community are derived from "Population Census, 1991: Geographical Distribution of the Population"; and Arkin, Magyar and Pillay's *The Indian South Africans*.

3. This is suggested in ANC internal evaluation reports, and claimed by ANC activists in Lenasia.

4. See K Moodley's "South African Indians: The Wavering Minority", in *Change in Contemporary South Africa*.

References

Arkin, A, K Maygar and G Pillay (eds) (1989) *The Indian South Africans* (Durban: Owen Burgess Publications).

Moodley, K (1975) "South African Indians: The Wavering Minority", Thompson, L and J Butler (eds) *Change in Contemporary South Africa* (Berkley: University of California Press).

Reynolds A (1994) *Elections '94 South Africa* (Cape Town: David Philip).

Schlemmer, L (1994) "Birth of Democracy", in *Indicator*, Vol 11, No 3.

Section 3

Identity Questions in the Coloured Communities

Chapter 8

Unveiling
the heart of fear

Ebrahim Rasool
MEC for Health and Social Services
Western Cape legislature

Coloureds are not so much racist as they fear non-racialism. The big unknowns for coloured people are non-racialism, freedom and equality. This is what confounds those, including coloured activists, who have fought all their lives for these values; that at the moment of victory, when the promised land is to be constructed, the wilderness is preferred.

Introduction

The debate about the coloured community dominated political discourse in the Western Cape before the historic April 1994 elections. Since then the debate has intensified as political parties and others try to come to grips with the outcome of the poll. The debate has spawned conservative, even right-wing coloured movements, the meeting of a coloured Forum, moves towards a coloured party – progressive or otherwise – and even debates about whether coloured should be spelt with a capital or small "c", whether the term should be used between inverted commas or whether it should be preceded by "so-called".

All of this, we are told, confirms a coloured consciousness and speaks of an emerging coloured identity. Many would frown at the emergence of this debate at the very moment that we have achieved the wherewithal to construct non-racialism, break down divisions and build a nation. It is clear that the ideal is again confounded by the reality.

Two options face those of us who share a sense of setback and who have sought to make sense of events. The first is to accept the reality as we perceive it and to act accordingly by getting into the language of "consciousness", "identity" and "our culture", by constructing formations (such as parties and forums) as demanded by that discourse and by strengthening the discourse with a mythology of values, norms, practices and stereotypes attributed to coloureds.

The second option is to interrogate the language or discourse, unveil it, reveal its assumptions, locate it in context and then, having identified its causal factors, develop an attitude and response towards it. Surely the latter option is preferable? What it is not is a route intended to quell the option that leads to formations – political or otherwise – within the coloured community. But if these are what is required, then they must be the result of a process of interrogating the discourse of a coloured consciousness and identity.

Origins of coloured disquiet

Disquiet within the coloured community surfaced during the 27 April election campaign. Much was made of the coloured factor in this election, and it was correctly identified as the critical issue in the outcome of the election in the Western Cape. This by itself was significant for coloured self-awareness.

During the campaign, the jubilation of the African National Congress (ANC) at the demise of apartheid and the imminence of non-racialism set off responses in the coloured community which were incomprehensible to ANC activists. How could anyone fear non-racialism, a philosophy that was universally and self-evidently good?

On the other hand, the National Party (NP) understood well that a long history of racial practice could not easily be erased from the coloured community. The NP knew that racism had not been an unstratified and equally applied practice in South Africa. In fact, the party used the historically unequal administration of racism to win support.

In politics all is fair and cowboys don't cry. But nation building and the non-racial project have suffered a setback and the Western Cape, by and large, remains racially divided, with these divisions even being entrenched.

Is there a coloured identity?

Is there a coloured identity? Is there even a coloured community? In apartheid parlance, coloured was everyone who was not white, African or clearly Indian. Under apartheid, this included a wide variety of people from a variety of ethnic, racial, cultural, social and linguistic backgrounds: Chinese, Malays, Khoi, San, Griqua and so on.

Within this broad coloured community, there is a profound sense of difference, even racism:

Kris (Christian) and *Slams* (Muslim); straight *hare* (hair) and *kroeskop* (curly head); English and Afrikaans; high society and worker; Walmer Estate *se mense* (people) and *die mense daar buite* (the people outside); *plaasjapie* (rural person) and city dweller; *Boesman* (Bushman), *Hotnot* (Hottentot) and so on.[1] One could ask what social or cultural cohesion exists? What common identity do all those called coloured share? What common features do they have? Is there a uniform consciousness?

Is there a coloured consciousness?

A cursory glance at a dictionary tells us that consciousness could mean "being conscious", possessing "the power of self-knowledge", an "internal perception" or "an aggregate of conscious states of a group of persons". In relation to the coloured community, we may well ask whether such self-knowledge exists or whether such an aggregate of conscious states is developing within this group of people. I would venture to say that there are certainly signs of an assertiveness within the coloured community, but it is not a gathering around binding, uniform, common, or even wholesome, "coloured" practices.

If anything, it is an aggregation around the perceived self-awareness of "the other" (blacks, Africans, "darkies"), even the perceived self-actualisation of the other. It is a fear that the other is reaching a level of consciousness and has the power to express that consciousness. Coloured consciousness and identity, rather than being self-aware, empowering and confident, are constructed fearfully, out of threat and opposition, and defined in negative relation to the other, not through a positive perception of the self.

Any self-awareness and consciousness that is developing in the coloured community takes place by way of actions which split that community: the Malays revel in their reawakened connection with Malaysia; the Griqua chiefs demand recognition and compensation; the Khoi and the San trace their history and lineages; and others identify their traditional lands. One may, therefore, speak more correctly of coloured communities and coloured identities as being the more positive, natural responses to the demise of apartheid's false unities and false divisions.

Is there a coloured disquiet?

One cannot dispute that, within sections of the coloured community, there has been a sense of disquiet, a fearful assertiveness, a laying down of claims, an appeal to coloureds as a group and a search for a fixed identity.

Does this constitute a cultural awakening, an ethnic stir, a racial identity, a linguistic awareness? Or is it a political response to a sense of socio-economic alienation and marginalisation within the process of constructing the South African nation?

Let us examine the form this disquiet has taken in the coloured community: coloured, Afrikaans-speaking, working-class people voted for the NP; conservative movements emerged in suburbs of Johannesburg and Cape Town to take up community issues in a militant manner; in student boycotts at the University of the Western Cape (UWC), coloured students openly expressed their dismay at no longer feeling at home at UWC; coloured members recently walked out of the ANC

Youth League in the Western Cape and formed their own organisation.

Focus group research carried out by the Community Agency for Social Enquiry (Case) gives credence to this sense of alienation from the political process in the country; this absence of someone who understands and speaks for coloureds. Case found that coloured people were "pessimistic about the future" and that most "feel insecure and scared about the future" and express it as a "fear of the unknown" (Everatt et al, 1994).

What is this fear of the unknown?

Some have said that this fear is a fear of Africans, and have gone so far as to accuse coloured people of racism. Racism certainly exists in significant doses among sections of the coloured community, but not necessarily more so than in many other sections of South African society.

Coloureds are not so much racist as they fear non-racialism. The big unknowns for coloureds are non-racialism, freedom and equality. This is what confounds those, including coloured activists, who have fought all their lives for these values; that at the moment of victory, when the promised land is to be constructed, the wilderness is preferred.

Coloureds were oppressed under apartheid, but they were also better placed in the hierarchy of apartheid. Non-racialism, freedom and equality usher in a future of competing equally for scarce resources, without preferential treatment and according to the same rules.

One such scarce resource is employment. Where yesterday the coloured labour preference area broadly secured jobs for coloured people, today's equality is perceived through affirmative action to provide jobs for Africans.

Housing is another area of contention. This was dramatically signalled in the housing occupations just before the election, coupled with whispers of Africans taking over all houses after the elections. That this has not materialised is now unimportant. The coloured community no longer has the guarantee to housing through the Group Areas Act. Again, the playing fields are level. One can mention other spheres of life where non-racialism, freedom and equality have evoked anxiety rather than liberty. These include access to welfare benefits and reserved places at UWC.

It is not as if the coloured people stand ignorant and unsympathetic in the face of what must be done in South Africa. It is that they perceive it will be done at their cost. The need among Africans is self-evident: coloured people see the squatter camps, they see the poor at the intersections and they know of the suffering through the media. More importantly, they know that something must be done. And, in the face of this vast disparity bequeathed by the NP, they fear they have already lost the race now that all South Africans begin from the same starting blocks. This is the heart of fear. It seems to be the material basis of the scramble for the new coloured identity and consciousness.

What is to be done?

Already there are many responses to this emerging phenomenon. But many of these are obscured by the impending local government elections and are often party-political responses aimed, not at unveiling the heart of fear, but rather at harnessing or even denying it.

Those who are trying to harness the fear have a head start, but they have commenced on a dangerous path by using a moment of *angst* for narrow political gain. At the end of the day, the anxiety that is sincerely felt by coloured people will remain at the service of those set on protecting essentially white privilege, leaving the material basis of life in coloured townships relatively unaltered. More than a year has passed since the elections and the NP, the majority party in the Western Cape government, has still not taken the coloured community further than it was on 27 April. Rather, the NP has embarked on elaborate dramas to speak to the heart of fear. This can only be described as apartheid from the grave.

A more benign response comes from those who operate at the levels of pure consciousness and identity. This approach is a misreading of the situation and can only assist in unravelling identity and consciousness into their component parts.

The key to the "coloured question" lies in translating non-racialism, freedom and equality into socio-economic programmes which visibly include the coloured community in ways which balance degrees of need with the claims of the majority group in the Western Cape. If, for example, health centres were only provided by the depth of need, we would only be building clinics in Crossroads and Khayelitsha for the next few years. The reality is that we are building them all over the province.

The crucial factor in this approach is the ANC. Only it has the non-racial, uplifting ethic to bring the coloured community into the nation and to provide comfort and confidence in the future. But for the ANC to do this, it has to undergo its own transformation at organisational and strategic levels, particularly in the Western Cape. It has to understand, for its own organisational practice, that non-racialism does not mean putting everyone into a melting pot and relying on the most organised being heard and attended to. This is important not only for policy formulation and implementation, but also for constructing its leadership and decision-making forums.

The problem in the Western Cape is that the ANC has been so confounded by the election result that it has not sought to think its way out of this position and to strategise anew. Strategising has been our traditional strength, and we need to return to it if we are to build a nation in diversity. ▲

Endnote

1. *Boesman* and *Hotnot* are used to make derogatory references to coloured people.

Reference

Everatt D, G Rapholo, C Lake and M Orkin (1994) *Finishing the Job? Deepening democracy and delivery benefits through successful local government elections* (Johannesburg: Case).

Chapter 9

Too long in the twilight [1]

Peter Marais
MEC for Local Government
Western Cape legislature

Unfortunately, the cultures of the Griqua and the Khoi-San were lost as a result of apartheid. So I aligned myself with another cultural group, the Afrikaner, with whom I found a home.

Introduction

Coloured people have been a twilight people for too long, and too long others have said what we are supposed to be, where we come from and where we should be politically. Nobody asks *us* where we want to be.

If there is no such person as a coloured, why has Idasa's Robert Mattes written an article about why coloureds voted for the National Party?[2] If we are blacks, one must say the NP won in the Western Cape with the black vote. That, at least, would be consistent. It is illogical to say the NP won the provincial election because of the coloured vote and then to add that coloureds do not exist. We are a people, just like everybody else in South Africa.

Under a black umbrella reside Xhosas, Zulus, Tswanas and Swahilis. They all call themselves black, thereby denoting an ethnic grouping. But they go on to say: "Although I am black, I am Zulu. Although I am black, I am Xhosa or Tswana." The whites say: "I am white, but I am also French or German or Afrikaans or English ..."[3]

Yet as soon as one refers to a coloured umbrella under which reside Griquas, Namas and Khoi-San, there are those who retort: "What is this new thing? Don't confuse me. Keep it simple; keep it black and white."

Some people claim to be black, but who are they fooling? They cannot speak a black language. They do not accept the chiefs of the blacks as their own. They do not accept the *indunas* (traditional leaders) as their rulers. They do not bow down when they see the king of the Zulus, Goodwill Zwelithini.

Personal matter

Identity is a deeply personal matter, one on which each individual, family and community must themselves decide. Individuals must find their own answers as to who they are, where they stand and what their allegiances are in relation to language, religion and culture.

My language, Afrikaans, provides the first indication of where I am located because many things flow from language. My religious affiliation is another feature of my identity. My traditions, the music I enjoy and even the jokes that make me laugh provide clues to my origins. While I do not find humour in the jokes of many other nations, I often roar with laughter on hearing jokes in the Cape because I am comfortable with that cultural milieu.

As a *bruin man* (brown man) of Griqua and Afrikaner descent, I do not wish to have another "bruin man" telling me who I am; or that I am nothing. On the contrary, I am something. I am a Griqua with Afrikaner blood. I am proud to say that I can trace my origins back to the Griqua, to Adam Kok and Niklaas Waterboer. And my Afrikaner ancestors were Dawid Slabbert Marais, Petrus Jakobus Marais and Dawid Ludwig Marais. I cannot help it if an Afrikaner fell in love with a Griqua girl. I was not responsible for deciding whom I should be.

Despite this Griqua-Afrikaner background, I regard myself as a *bruin* Afrikaner. The reference to *bruin* simply indicates that my ethnic origins are Griqua and Khoi-San. Unfortunately, the cultures of the Griqua and the Khoi-San were lost as a result of apartheid. So I aligned myself with another cultural group, the Afrikaner, with whom I found a home.

A minority group

The American negro comes from Africa, and black Americans come to Africa to find their roots. Yet they never stay because they have adopted a new culture. They return to the United States because they no longer fit in with African culture. The acculturation process cannot be halted; one culture always learns from the next.

That is why I assert that *bruin mense* (brown people) are a minority group. Those who claim to be black give up, in effect, the possibility of being recognised as a minority group. The view of the United Nations (UN) on minority groups is relevant here. In a 1979 study on the rights of persons belonging to ethnic, religious and linguistic minorities, author Francesco Cappatorti says:

> A minority group is a group numerically inferior to the rest of the population of
> the state, in a non-dominant position, whose members – being nationals of the

state – possess ethnic, religious or linguistic characteristics differing from the rest of the population, and show, if only implicitly, a sense of solidarity directing towards preserving their culture or their traditions or their religion or a language (1979: Paragraph 568).

The report says further that those who fulfil such criteria have the right to be recognised as a group if they so wish:

Membership of a group is determined, not according to a law on the basis of precise criteria, but on the basis of a formally expressed wish of the individual. In Romania, for example, the law on the status of the nationalities provides that each citizen is authorised to establish his own nationality. Any interference by any authority in this matter is prohibited and the official organs are obliged to accept the citizen's declaration (Paragraph 569).

The implication of this is that no one in this country can, just because he or she has a brown skin, tell another person with a brown skin who that person should be.

The law on race classification defined us in negative terms: if you were not black, white or Asian, then you were coloured. No wonder we are debating who we are! But I know who I am, and nobody will convince me otherwise. I am easily recognisable. I dare anybody to look at me and say I am a white man, or that I am Indian, or Japanese. No one would say that I am Zulu: my language is Afrikaans, not Zulu. To see people as coming from different races is not racist: race has nothing to do with racism.

Finally, it is ironic that at this conference, English is being used to discuss issues relating to coloured people in the Western Cape when 80 percent of coloureds are Afrikaans speaking. To insult Afrikaans is to insult the overwhelming majority of *bruin mense*.   ▲

Endnotes

1. The bulk of this paper was delivered in Afrikaans to the Idasa conference on "National Unity and the Politics of Diversity: The Case of the Western Cape".

2. Mattes's article, "Why coloureds voted Nat", appeared in *Weekend Argus*, 19 August 1995.

3. Editors' note: Throughout the book, the term black is used to refer to all those discriminated against under apartheid. However, the author of this paper uses black to denote African people and specifically argues that coloured people should not be referred to as black. As terminology is an integral part of Marais's argument, this has not been changed.

References

Cappatorti, F (ed) (1979) *Study on the Rights of Persons Belonging to Ethnic, Religious and Linguistic Minorities*, United Nations document No E78, Vol 14.

Chapter 10

Breaking down
the borders

Julian Sonn
Deputy Director & Psychologist
Centre for Cognitive Development

As brown people, we have internalised the pervasive white

racist message that "white is right" and "West is best". This

has encouraged brown communities to distance themselves

from their African origins and seek greater identification

with whites.

Introduction

Borders – both physical and mental – have long been part of the South Africa story. I grew up in Queenstown, an English colonial town in a part of South Africa that is often referred to as "the border" – the border, to my mind, between the more Europeanised part of the country and the more African part. To be more specific about my origins, I was born in Nuwerus, which was called a coloured location. Situated between the predominantly African location, or *lokaai*, and the mainly white Queenstown, Nuwerus itself was a border.

In subsequent years I have often found myself on "the border". My work has focused on how South Africans can negotiate the many borders, or barriers, that exist as a result of the past. In our quest to create a unified vision, we need to uncover the different experiences lived on the different sides of the borders as we grew up.

As we engage in the challenging and exciting task of defining our new emerging nation, I am often touched by the strong sense of hope and human decency I experience in South Africa at present. As we define ourselves as people in and of Africa, it is my wish that we should embrace the strong sense of spirituality, community and respect for all people that has always been an integral part of the African ethos.

I want to share my vision of a non-racial, non-sexist, non-classist, inclusive democracy and urge those who are serious about making this vision a reality to attend to and confront all the barriers to achieving inclusivity. These barriers include sexism, white racism, classism and other forms of oppression. The different forms of internalised oppression must also be attended to and unlearned. Now that political liberation is becoming a reality in South Africa, the need for psychological, economic, social and cultural liberation is becoming more evident.

In discussing the politics of differences, it is essential to clarify who we are, where we are from and how we want to be seen by others. At issue is the interaction between the personal need for a clear sense of identity and aspects of the cultural context in which this liberating process occurs, while keeping in mind political and social goals.

> We are the dispersed Khoi
> scattered reflections
> in the arteries of Africa
> We are the tributaries
> of many rivers merged
> yet still flowing
> towards a new destiny
>
> Brian Williams (1994) *Scattered Reflections.*

Clarity about identity

Most South Africans are now engaged in defining and re-defining themselves. This is a healthy process that provides an important, if fleeting, opportunity to create a unified vision that is based on the wondrous heterogeneity that characterises our society.

This process is apparent in all communities. President Nelson Mandela provides a good example of someone who is clear about his Xhosa roots and equally clear about his commitment to inclusivity and reconciliation. Some Afrikaans-speaking white South Africans are also saying: "We are *Afrikaanse Suid-Afrikaners*; we are *Afrikaanses*; we are *Afrikaners*; we are *boere*". Others maintain: "We are South Africans or Africans."

Similarly, in the brown communities I often define myself as both a black South African and as a brown South African. I am aware that some choose to define themselves as black, Africans, South Africans, coloureds or "so-called coloureds" or "those previously classified as coloured".

English-speaking white South Africans are grappling with their sense of connection and loyalty to both Britain and South Africa. They talk about carrying two passports and their choice to live in and identify with South Africa.

Jewish South Africans often grapple with historical exclusion and oppression, while at the same time recognising that their white skins have secured them privileges and other commonalities with white oppression.

In my work I am fortunate to listen to this important process of grappling with issues of ethnic and national identity, and I am convinced it is an essential aspect of creating national unity.

The use of concepts

I prefer to use the term "ethnic identity" when referring to our ancestry, so as not to perpetuate the use of racial identity and the erroneous assumption that "race" is a viable construct. But while racism is a legacy and a reality, the construct "race", denoting primarily skin colour, is devoid of substance. Ashley Montagu (1974: 14, 62) states that "race" is an utterly erroneous and meaningless construct. Biological variation is continuous and does not conform to discrete packages labelled race. He argues further, and I agree, that as "race" is based on unexamined facts and unjustifiable generalisations, it is better that the term be dropped altogether. Yet in countless books and articles, terms such "racial groups", "multi-racial schools" and "inter-racial marriages" are used. By using such terminology, racist thinking is sometimes fostered.

I use the terms "black", "brown" and "white" as racist terms to talk about the legacy and reality of racism. I also use the term "black" to refer to all those people who have been excluded and discriminated against on the basis of colour. "African" is sometimes used interchangeably with "black" to refer to those South Africans whose forebears were solely from Africa and who have maintained a distinct history and identity. My ancestors, for example, are from both Europe and Africa.

The use of language to describe individuals or groups is a powerful social tool that can be used to value or disparage. We need to constantly consider the implications of the terms we use and agree to use alternatives where appropriate. Although the concept "race" is devoid of substance, the social reality and political disparities that are related to racism continue to affect our current reality.

It is therefore essential that we deal specifically with racism and its ongoing effect on life in South Africa, keeping in mind that a non-racial society is our ultimate vision. In a non-racial society, colour will not determine access to power and resources, and will hopefully become less significant. This is clearly not the case at present. Vast inequalities are closely tied to skin colour as a direct consequence of racist policies. Racial categorisation is also going to be necessary during this period of transformation to redress the inequities and to implement affirmative action programmes and other strategies to achieve inclusiveness at all levels.

Racial categories will also be important in census figures to measure how far we have progressed toward inclusiveness and social justice. A tendency to support the myth of colour blindness often mitigates against this short-term use of racial categorisation.

Ethnic identity

I use "ethnic identity" to refer to a sense of individual and group identity based on the perception that one shares a common heritage and a common historical experience. This sense of historical experience is an essential element in the current discourse about identity. It is in this sense that I identify both with my African identity and with the brown communities. The brown communities share an African, Asian and European heritage, coupled with a common historical experience.

It is often helpful to start with oneself in this discussion about ethnic identity. Clearly the question "Who I am?" has never been a simple one. Until recently, it was taboo in the brown communities to discuss who our forebears were. When we talk about our Khoi-Khoi and Khoi-San roots, older members of my family often react strongly, saying: "Jy kan miskien 'n Boesman wees maar ek is beslis nie een nie." ("You can be a Bushman, but I am definitely not one.")

Apparently, my paternal grandfather's mother was a Xhosa woman who worked in Carnarvon. His father was a Jewish merchant who never fully recognised him as his son. My grandfather, like so many blacks, grew up with his mother's mother on a farm.

My father's mother was a Pieterse, another proud and dignified family from Carnarvon with Xhosa and Dutch ancestry. I know less about my mother's background, except that she was a Klein and also from Carnarvon. It is with pride that I acknowledge the ability of my grandparents and parents to survive and thrive, often under difficult circumstances.

I accept my European heritage and realise that I can draw on both my European and African ancestry. But I do not accept that part of the European heritage which represents the exploitation and dehumanisation of other people. I am also aware of not knowing much about my heritage and I am aware how painful this often is in brown communities. Our European forefathers also contributed to our oppression by rejecting our African and Asian ancestors.

In our search to know our essence as South Africans, it is helpful to talk as honestly as we can about our particular heritage and about the historical and social realities we have experienced. The aim is not to glorify a sometimes difficult past or to foster a *volkstaat* (nation-state) mentality, but to realise that, as children of Africa, we have a lot to be proud of. An essential part of our liberation will continue to be reclaiming all aspects of our past and the past of Africa and Africans.

Identity formation

Various factors have contributed to the development of separate communities for brown South Africans and have influenced our experiences, attitudes and sense of identity. These include the legacy of slavery, the influence of religious groups and the role of missionaries.

The influence of the Khoi-Khoi and Khoi-San people contributed both to our sense of identity and to the difficulties of acknowledging aspects of our identity. The Khoi are usually presented in a negative light: as lazy, dirty thieves in the history books. We often internalised these negative messages and felt insulted to acknowledge these aspects of our ancestry. The genocide and dispersement of the Khoi further complicated our acknowledgement of this aspect of our heritage.

In other parts of the country, the experiences and origins of the brown communities were influenced by the demographics, politics and history of that particular region. These brown communities are, by definition, heterogeneous.

The colonial and apartheid eras complicated the process of self-definition. A false dichotomy between black and white South Africans was created. The racist policies and attitudes often defined all South Africans from Africa and Asia as black and all South Africans with more obvious European ancestry as white. This crude distinction often obscures the heterogeneity of all South Africans. The government also used and abused identity to implement its unfortunate policies. Differences were both emphasised and crudely manipulated to achieve political ends.

The practices of successive governments, particularly the creation of separate residential areas, contributed to the development of secondary cultural characteristics that influenced a sense of separate identities. Prior to the implementation of the Group Areas Act, South Africans lived closer together in many parts of the country and often experienced a strong sense of community. This aspect of our history provides an example of our ability to live together.

The preferential treatment we received in the brown communities relative to our African brothers and sisters also contributed to a sense of being "better than", which I define as internalised white racism. This does not mean that we did not experience the harshness of oppression in the brown communities. On the contrary, the racist system that perpetuated the notion that "West is best" and "white is right" discriminated severely against all those who did not meet the bizarre, racist standards of "whiteness".

White racism, such an integral part of the culture of South Africa, consistently influenced brown communities. Our ancestors internalised the same messages heard by whites: that white is better than brown, and brown is better than black. The lack of recognition and the rejection experienced by our forebears, usually by their white father, is an example of the influence and pain of racism of those "better than, less than" messages. It is also helpful to share some conditions and factors that will facilitate the process of self-definition and liberation.

Essential elements in our liberation

Two processes continue to be essential aspects of my liberation: accepting that I am an African and recognising the substantial contributions of Africans to all civilisations. When I realised that the Egyptian civilisation was a black African civilisation, I was proud. When I started reading about the thriving civilisations of Mali, Songhay and Ghana, long before Europe emerged from its slumber, I was delighted. When I discovered that Greece was a colony of Egypt and Ethiopia, and that most of the Greek philosophers I was told about actually studied in Egypt, I was amazed.

The denial of the strong and pervasive influence of Africa in the world also angered me. Part of our oppression has been the distortion of our history and the entire history of African people. Western nations assumed that Africa had no history and that Africans were without a significant past. We were not told about the civilisations of the Khoi-Khoi and Zulu people. Their stories were distorted to support the racist belief that "West is best". In fact, his-story was often the story of white men and their wars and exploitation.

Today, it is our challenge to tell our stories and to listen intently to the stories of our mothers and fathers. Our self-esteem is locked up in an honest discovery of who we are and where we come from. Knowing our essence is one route to greater self-esteem, and self-esteem fosters an ability to embrace other people and participate in nation building. Cultural affirmation is essential for the development of self-esteem to counter the devaluing that has been such a consistent part of colonialism and racism.

We must talk about apartheid and colonialism – not to blame, but to release the strong feelings associated with those forms of oppression and to liberate ourselves. When talking about colonialism and apartheid, the underlying theme of white racism must be attended to. It is paradoxical that all of us need to talk clearly and honestly about the various ways we have been injured by racism in order to create a non-racial society and liberate ourselves.

The creation and defence of group privileges at institutional and cultural levels usually underlie the domination of one racial or gender group over the other. Thus it is helpful to distinguish between earned and unearned privileges (McIntosh, 1987). Unearned privileges – or the automatic and often invisible ways in which whites derived benefits – are at the heart of racial oppression and taint all white South Africans. The fight against racism is not only about individual attitudes, but also about group interests, values and power.

Racism will continue to mar our relationships with each other because it operates as a strategy to divide and conquer. It sets groups of people against others and makes it difficult to perceive their common interests. Racism limits our horizons and distorts our perceptions of the possibilities of change. It makes us abandon our visions of solidarity and it robs us of our dreams of community (Sherover-Marcuse, 1988). It is only by expressing the anger, crying the tears and listening to one another that we will heal the deep wounds left by these oppressive thoughts, feelings and behaviours.

Distinguishing between old-fashioned and modern racism (Batts, 1982) is helpful and acknowledges the changes in the manifestations of racism in South Africa at present. Modern racism involves covert and subtle ways in which discrimination and exclusion continues – although based on reasons unrelated to race. For example, implementing affirmative action poorly or increasing entrance fees at public facilities now that blacks are allowed to enter can be forms of modern racism.

Levels of racism

Racism operates on several different levels:
- *Personal level:*
  At this level, racism is reflected in personal values, beliefs, thoughts and feelings. These attitudes are usually based on misinformation that is associated with emotions. The belief that black people are dangerous is an example of personal-level racism. At this level, racism can be conscious or unconscious.
- *Inter-personal level:*
  The personal values, beliefs and attitudes we hold affect the way in which we interact with others who are not only different, but who are also judged as "less than". So, for example, if you believe that black people are dangerous, it is likely you will be cautious and afraid when relating to black people.
- *Institutional level:*
  White racism, or the assumption that "white is right", has been part of the customs, traditions, laws, rules and regulations of the South African society since the first contact between the white explorers and colonists and the indigenous people of the land. All the institutions are therefore steeped in the racist tradition that tends to devalue that which is

African and Asian. This is exacerbated by the general lack of knowledge about African philososphy, beliefs and languages. Declaring English and Afrikaans as the official languages of South Africa was an example of institutionalised racism.

- *Cultural level:*
  This level of racism is perhaps the most profound in its effects, but is often hidden. Being like Europeans is usually regarded as proper and beautiful. This attitude seems ingrained in the media, advertising, movies, schools and in some places of worship.

Racism, sexism and all the other forms of oppression usually influence the group targeted as "less than" others. The "less than" message is internalised and believed. Internalised oppression – the unhealed mistreatment and negative messages about a person's group over time – must also be attended to and unlearned. Much of this behaviour is functional when the oppression is real. Being subservient, for example, had survival value. Now that we can play our rightful role, however, internalised oppression will only continue to undermine our effectiveness.

Believing, and sometimes unconsciously acting on, oppressive messages that we are "less than" is closely tied to two particular forms of internalised oppression: internalised white racism and delegated white racism.

Internalised white racism is another form of oppression to be addressed by those who have been targeted as "less than" whites. "Brown racism" or "coloured racism" is often raised, but it is important to make a few important distinctions. As brown people, we have internalised the pervasive white racist message that "white is right" and "West is best". This has encouraged brown communities to distance themselves from their African origins and seek greater identification with whites.

These false perceptions have political and personal consequences. In our families we ridiculed those who did not meet the white standards of beauty and propriety; we tended to devalue that which is African. The tragedy of internalised white racism by brown people continues to be that we deny parts of our history, heritage and ourselves. The psychological implications of accepting the notions of European superiority must be addressed consistently.

Unfortunately, whites fostered and promoted the notion that the brown communities were a "little better" than African communities while at the same time rejecting and severely discriminating against brown people, starting with genocide of the Khoi people. I take exception to the tendency to focus exclusively on the internalised white racism of brown people without a concomitant emphasis on the impact of white racism. After all, white racism continues to complicate our relationships with each other as South Africans and also creates an abnormal society where whites usually "have" and black and brown people usually "don't have".

Delegated white racism, which focuses on how whites have delegated some of their power to certain willing black people, is closely related to internalised white racism. This delegated power often involved blacks serving on councils, boards and in pseudo-parliamentary structures such as homeland governments and the tricameral parliament.

The delegation of racism was used to maintain control, divide black communities and bestow unearned privileges. The power delegated by whites and the attendant privileges were seductive to those historically excluded from power. Unfortunately, sometimes there was not only an assumption that the power was real, but also a belief that its recipients were "better than" their other black brothers and sisters.

To promote psychological and cultural liberation, a climate must be created in which all of us can comfortably speak about all aspects of ourselves. Our differences and similarities must be recognised, understood and appreciated. Such a multi-cultural strategy must also attend to all the barriers – such as racism and sexism. Since an unfortunate consequence of racism has been the devaluing of that which is African, it is essential that we reclaim our African heritage while also acknowledging our Asian and European heritages. It is in this spirit that I am excited about making this a truly inclusive country and seeing that beauty and virtue are appreciated in all colours.   ▲

References

Batts, V (1982) "Theory Related to Specific Issues", in *Transactional Analysis Journal*, Vol 12, No 3.

Diop, CA (1959) *The Cultural Unity of Africa* (Chicago: Third World Press).

Diop, CA (1974) *The African Origin of Civilisation: Myth and Reality* (Chicago: Lawrence Hill Books).

McIntosh, P (1986) "Male and White Privilege", unpublished paper.

Montagu, A (1974) *Man's Most Dangerous Myth: The Fallacy of Race* (New York: Oxford Press).

Sherover-Marcuse, R (1980) "Unlearning Racism Workshops", unpublished paper.

Van Sertina, I (ed) (1985) *African Presence in Early Europe* (New Brunswick: Transaction Books).

Williams, B (1994) *Scattered Reflections* (Cape Town: Olmic Press).

Williams, C (1974) *The Destruction of Black Civilisation: Great Issues of Race from 4500 BC to 2000 AD* (Chicago: Third World Press).

Section 4

Affirmative Action and Equity

Chapter 11

The RDP and affirmative action

Howard Gabriels
Special Adviser to the Minister without Portfolio
Reconstruction and Development Programme Office

In building a single nation we must recognise the different cultures, languages and religions in our society. What makes us different, our diversity, is a strength upon which we must build our future. On the other hand, the fear of minorities can also destroy us.

The Reconstruction and Development Programme (RDP) Office has been asked to address the question: "What is the RDP doing about affirmative action?" I believe this is the wrong question. It reflects a common misunderstanding about the RDP, which sees Minister without Portfolio Jay Naidoo as being solely responsible for the RDP. It is important to clarify that the government as a whole, under the leadership of the president, is responsible for implementing the RDP. We should rather ask: "What are we doing about affirmative action and equity to implement the goals and principles of the RDP?"

Nation building and reconciliation

One of the key principles of the RDP is nation building. The president, since the inception of the government of national unity, has personally driven a process of reconciliation in our country – reaching out to people across the length and breadth of the country who have certain fears of the new democracy we are building now. This process of bringing together people across the spectrum of our society is fundamental to the achievement of the political stability we have today.

Shortly before the April 1994 election, many believed that it would be impossible to achieve a peaceful political settlement in South Africa. Many feared that, when members of the Afrikaner Weestandsbeweging (AWB) invaded Bophuthatswana, the dream of a new South Africa was shattered. A number of people went out and bought boxes of tinned food and candles in case the country was plunged into chaos after the election. It is important to remind ourselves that this was the context in which the president embarked on a path of reconciliation to address the fears of minorities.

In building a single nation we must recognise the different cultures, languages and religions in our society. What makes us different, our diversity, is a strength upon which we must build our future. On the other hand, the fear of minorities can also destroy us. The history of South Africa teaches us that we cannot sustain our society on privileges for minorities. While we must address legitimate fears, there can be no doubt that racism, or any sense of superiority based on race, will be combated.

The role of the RDP Office

The RDP Office's role is to allocate resources to projects and programmes in line with the RDP's principles and criteria. For this purpose, the RDP Fund was created in 1994. Initially, the fund was resourced from savings in the budgets of the various departments. Departments then approach the RDP Fund to introduce projects and programmes which meet RDP criteria. The onus to implement the RDP thus lies with the whole government – the national line departments and provinces – and not only with the minister.

The RDP Fund could be seen as a tool to effect change. Its goals, as defined in the RDP White Paper, are to:
- direct government spending and the entire budget to new priorities;
- encourage institutional reform and public sector restructuring;
- redeploy the civil service in line with the new priorities;
- kickstart the Presidential Lead Projects and launch new programmes; and
- redirect expenditure away from capital consumption expenditure and towards capital expenditure.

Regarding the RDP projects, we have insisted that a business plan is drawn up for each project. The criteria applied in these business plans are vital in addressing affirmative action. In addition to the normal requirements of the business plan – such as progress against budgets and cash flow – we ask departments and provinces to state at the outset what their plans are to ensure the participation of small business, to highlight what training will be introduced, how many jobs will be created and how many women will be employed and to consult the community which will benefit from the project.

We have experienced many problems, for example with tender procedures and the access of small, micro- and medium enterprises (SMMEs) to tender for projects. In some instances, the consultation process contributed to the delays in the implementation of some projects. Consultation and participation by communities in the development process must enhance delivery not hinder it. Despite these problems, many projects are successfully addressing these issues and a sound partnership is being built between communities and government.

Over the past few weeks we have heard powerful voices arguing that we must "go for growth". We should forget about redistribution and other important tasks such as the transformation of the civil service. Of course, we must place emphasis on growth. We must place maximum effort on introducing policies that will promote the competitive edge of our companies, which must compete in the global economy. Emphasis must be placed on employment creation. On the other hand, we must address basic needs in our communities.

The 1994 October Household Survey is the first official sample undertaken by the Central Statistical Service with the specific aim of making information available in terms of the RDP. The survey found that 100 percent of white urban households compared to 98 percent of Indian and coloured and 80 percent of African households have access to refuse removal. In rural areas of the Eastern Cape, 34 percent of people do not have access to sanitation. This means people do not have access to a toilet, not even a pit latrine. These are the realities we must address. The manner in which we address them must be fiscally responsible and promote economic growth.

Transformation of the civil service

The transformation of the civil service is one of the most crucial tasks of the government. The civil service has to be made truly representative of all the people in South Africa. We have inherited a civil service dominated by white males. A significant number of senior black civil servants have been engaged during the first year of the new government, and the first woman was recently appointed as a director general.

During 1994, the 11 different administrations were brought together into a single civil service in 33 national departments and nine provinces. This process of rationalisation will continue as the alignment of conditions of service are negotiated with employee representatives.

The RDP White Paper calls for the redeployment of civil servants and a continuous evaluation of all posts: "Posts which are not consistent with the new priorities should be removed." Many areas, such as grading systems and the wage gap between top and bottom, need to be addressed. In 1994, major steps were taken in this direction. At present, the Ministry of the Public Service and Administration is embarking on a comprehensive training programme to develop the skills of the management echelon of the civil service.

In the process of transforming the public service, there are many challenges facing the government. These include improving conditions of employment, developing career paths and developing a comprehensive training programme. There is also the need to restrict the growth of the number of public servants employed in the civil service and to shift the civil service to a performance culture.

Many of these challenges are also confronting the private sector, both employers and trade unions.

Affirmative action and business

It is often asked what business is doing about affirmative action. Too often this is measured by counting the number of black faces on the board of directors. This is a fundamental mistake. We should ask a company what human resources policies it has in place. What is its buying policy? How is it engaging with SMMEs when buying for the company? What are firms doing for its workers who cannot read and write? Are firms unlocking opportunities for employees at all levels of the company? How these policies are implemented is vital to enhance the competitive edge of the companies.

Another important area to be addressed is the ownership of businesses in South Africa. Ownership is concentrated in white hands. Currently, the Ministry of Trade and Industry is developing a competition policy and already a White Paper has been adopted by parliament on the promotion of small and medium enterprises.

The implementation of these policies must promote local economic development (LED). LED strategies aim to restructure local economies, promote neighbourhood development, expand employment opportunities, enhance the local tax base and mobilise resources from the public and private sectors as well as the community.

A few years ago, a consultant related a story about a company executive who had the vision that a contribution could be made in the sphere of education. He requested the consultant to find 10 matriculants who could be assisted to obtain university educations. The consultant then asked the executive for the company's employee records and found at least 10 labourers employed who had matrics and were capable of attending university.

In general, we are not concerned with the vast number of company workers who cannot read and write. We seem too obsessed with the management echelons in the company. The RDP is not just concerned with the social responsibility programmes of companies but also with industrial restructuring.

The essential point I am trying to make is that affirmative action is not about a selection policy concerned only with the number of black managers. We should be concerned with opening up opportunities to employees at all levels of companies. Companies should find ways to assist those employees who qualify to obtain housing, become literate and generally improve their skills. The acceleration of training at all levels of a company is an urgent task.

The apartheid system placed us in racial compartments. We must break out of these. Division in our society means that we are ignorant about each other. One of the biggest dangers is that we create stereotypes. We need to take very deliberate steps to combat whatever prejudices we may have.

The spatial dimension of affirmative action

The spatial framework we inherited is characterised by the uneven development and inequality within cities and between provinces as well as townships which lack basic infrastructure and services. In some parts of the country, extreme poverty exists. Provincial governments have an important task to develop plans that will address these needs. To ensure co-operation between provinces, government has established the Forum for Effective Planning and Development (FEPD), which is co-chaired by the Minister of Land Affairs and the Minister without Portfolio, and includes all provincial MECs for development planning. The FEPD's task is to develop a national development framework within which provincial development plans are located.

The Urban and Rural Development strategies proposed by the government aim to reverse apartheid spatial planning and spell out a coherent framework for redeveloping our rural areas, towns and cities.

The Constitution also established the Financial and Fiscal Commission whose task is to develop minimum standards across all provinces. It will also develop a formula for revenue sharing between provinces which will guide budgetary allocations.

Over the coming months and years, resources will be allocated in a manner that will promote more even development of all provinces and more equitable allocation of resources between provinces.

Conclusion

I have argued that affirmative action should not be reduced to a selection policy aimed at replacing some white faces with black faces on the boards of directors and at managerial levels. Affirmative action should be addressing the opening of opportunities at all levels of companies and should not create more apartheid walls between the "haves" and the "have nots".

Perhaps affirmative action is an inappropriate term to describe the intention in South Africa to correct the legacy of apartheid. The Afrikaans term *regstellende aksie* or corrective action is a more appropriate description of the intention. ▲

Chapter 12

Motives, methods and milieux [1]

Philip Black
Professor of Economics
University of Cape Town

Valerie Flanagan
Researcher
Food and Allied Workers' Union

Companies may be more willing to invest their time and money in human resource policies when they are certain that their competitors will also engage in them, and when they believe that those competitors will ultimately face the same costs, should those policies fail.

Introduction

Affirmative action has been a dominant feature of the South African economy over the past few years. It is being widely applied in both the private and public sectors and has become an integral part of the debate on the new political economy of South Africa.

We are currently involved in a major research project involving a survey of small and large institutions in the private and public sectors. We had hoped to be able to report here on some of our findings but the response thus far has been limited. Nonetheless, we would like to share with you some of the findings that we do have and also to discuss some of the hypotheses that we are trying to test.

We address three important questions: why firms adopt affirmative action strategies, how affirmative action is applied in practice and the external factors that influence it. First, however, it is worth spelling out precisely what we mean by the term "affirmative action".

What is affirmative action?

Not every appointment of a so-called disadvantaged employee necessarily constitutes an act of affirmation as it is ordinarily understood. In fact, the managing director of a large group of companies recently intimated this much, arguing that the corporate human resource policy was based on the principle of appointing the "best person for the job".

He attributed the appointment of increasing numbers of women and black men to various technical and managerial positions, and the allocation of more resources to the training of these employees, to an acute shortage of suitable personnel. He also indicated that potential candidates were evaluated on the basis of overall competencies, rather than merely in terms of their academic or technical qualifications.

In addition, the shortage of qualified workers in rural areas has forced companies in many cases to select employees from available pools of disadvantaged candidates and, where none has been available, they have tended to invest in external training programmes with an eye to ensuring a future. This is particularly evident in Mpumalanga and Northern Province, where companies draw attention to their support of local schools and other educational institutions where they provide funds for the acquisition of textbooks and scientific materials.

South Africa has experienced skills shortages for many years. Our ratio of managers to workers is currently about one to 70 and is expected to reach one to 110 by the year 2000. The equivalent ratio in many other countries is one manager for every 25 workers (Kemp, 1993: 12). It is estimated that the shortage of managerial staff in South Africa will rise to 100 000 over the next decade, while a shortage of some 200 000 technically trained personnel is expected to develop over the same period (Roodt, 1992: 15). These estimates suggest a need both to search for available talent in traditionally neglected labour pools and to invest in the development of appropriate skills (O'Regan and Thompson, 1993).

Presumably there are other reasons why South African employers have recently begun appointing increasing numbers of women and black men to important managerial and other supervisory positions. These are essentially "affirmative action appointments", that is, appointment or promotion of educationally disadvantaged employees who, on the whole, are technically less productive, or less able to fulfil the "particular" requirements of the "job", than the best available advantaged candidates. In other words, it is assumed here that an affirmative action appointee, by definition, is not the "best person for the job", at least not in the short run. We shall return to this point.

A firm practising affirmative action, as defined here, will have to incur additional labour costs, such as productivity foregone in the short run, additional time and money spent searching for, training and supervising disadvantaged employees, and resources allocated towards maintaining motivational levels among advantaged personnel (Black, 1993). These costs are presumably weighed against the expected benefits of affirmative action, some of which are discussed below.

Rationales

Some employers may be practising affirmative action because they feel "socially responsible" and are consequently pursuing the so-called public interest, taking it upon themselves to redress the socio-economic imbalances caused by past policies of racial discrimination (Black, 1993). Thus motivated, these employers are prepared to carry the additional costs referred to above, partly to make up for the limited access that blacks had to the sources of human capital formation during the apartheid era.

However, from the point of view of an individual firm, the success of such a policy will depend on what its rivals do. If rival firms are not prepared to incur the additional costs associated with affirmative action, a firm taking on those costs may lose its competitive edge and run the risk of financial ruin. Thus there is a limit to the extent to which employers can pursue the public interest.

On the other hand, it is also possible that new perspectives and agreements arising out of industrial policy-making forums composed of labour, business, government and other relevant stakeholders may persuade companies to implement affirmative action policies sooner rather than later. This is particularly likely when responsibility for the success or failure of these policies can be spread across those groups within the forum which designed them by consensus. Companies may be more willing to invest their time and money in human resource policies when they are certain that their competitors will also engage in them, and when they believe that those competitors will ultimately face the same costs, should those policies fail.

Of course, there is a fine line between acting in the public interest and enhancing one's own reputation within the broader community. There may indeed be a non-pecuniary gain to be had from launching a highly visible affirmative action programme. The initial impetus for adopting affirmative action may have been world-wide condemnation of racial discrimination and its resultant negative impact on the reputation of firms (forced into) practising it. The moral pressure on foreign-owned firms during the 1980s to adopt certain "ethical" codes of behaviour, such as the Sullivan principles, may have encouraged local firms to do likewise. The point is that an improvement in a firm's reputation induced by affirmative action may well outweigh any corresponding short-term cut in its profit.

Similarly, employers may select a human resource policy which they believe will be endorsed by a particular labour organisation, such as the Congress of South African Trade Unions, or by a particularly popular political leader. An example of the latter case is Archbishop Desmond Tutu's endorsement of milling company Sasko's "Green Areas" programme, a literacy and numeracy training programme. This kind of consideration may result in companies adopting high-profile public relations campaigns aimed at signalling their willingness to implement investment-friendly contemporary social policies.

A related reason for adopting affirmative action policies involves what Vincent Maphai (1989) calls "reaction qualifications". These refer to individual abilities or characteristics with the potential to elicit positive reactions from "third parties", which ultimately may have a positive impact on the *overall* profitability of the firm (Akerlof, 1976; 1980). Thus, in addition to their formal academic or technical qualifications, the "reaction qualifications" of potential candidates are considered by employers, with a view to the contribution they can make to realising the overall objectives of the institution.

In other words, the additional costs involved in appointing a disadvantaged candidate, which pertain mostly to the job itself, may be more than offset by certain benefits arising from the individual's reaction qualifications. The new appointee may be best able to utilise emerging black consumer markets, secure new government contracts, resolve conflicts between management and (predominantly black) labour, and help the company to compete effectively on international markets (Black, 1993; 1995). The relevant criterion is therefore the appointment of the "best person for the *institution*", rather than the "best person for the job".

On the other hand, such appointments may be viewed as mere window-dressing and thus turn out to be counter-productive. They may not, in fact, impress "third parties" and may also undermine morale and productivity within the company, thus ultimately adding to the costs of the operation (Madi, 1993; Patel, 1993).

Applications

It is of some importance to know whether companies participate in, or support, external programmes aimed at the advancement of historically disadvantaged persons, or whether their efforts are mainly limited to their own recruitment and training policies.

Support for external initiatives, for example, academic support programmes at schools, universities and other training institutions may be rooted in a belief in their effectiveness in levelling the proverbial playing-field. Where companies prefer to do their own training, the reason may well be that educational institutions are incapable of producing enough individuals possessing the kind of skills or competencies required in the job market.

It is important also to know the managerial, supervisory and other levels at which affirmative action appointments are made, as well as the relevant divisions and job contents. Of equal importance is whether companies change their grading policies and job descriptions when appointing disadvantaged employees to particular posts. Such changes may well enable employers to accommodate appropriate "reaction qualifications" and thus secure the attendant benefits.

There is a further need to consider the relative importance of selection criteria used when affirmative action appointments are made, and to determine whether they have changed over time, how they are verified, and whether candidates are tested for potential. Such information may have important implications for the role that education plays in preparing potential candidates for the job market.

If criteria other than formal academic and technical qualifications feature prominently in the selection process, our findings may well challenge the prevailing belief in the efficacy and efficiency of the current education system and, in particular, the crucial screening role that it is supposed to play.

External factors

The external economic environment within which a firm operates may well affect its ability to implement affirmative action programmes. Human resource policies are presumably sensitive to economic upswings and downswings, or to structural factors such as weather changes and new international trade agreements arising from South Africa's participation in the General Agreement on Trade and Tariffs (Gatt) and membership of the World Trade Organisation. However, the effect of these influences may vary between different economic sectors, industries and individual firms.

It might be argued, on the one hand, that an externally induced profit squeeze would undermine a company's ability to absorb the additional costs associated with affirmative action, and vice versa. On the other hand, such downward economic pressure might force management to engage in more frequent interaction with its employees, partly to secure better co-operation and an increase in labour productivity. The consequence could be that employees at grassroots level become more meaningfully informed of company policies and strategies, with the result that a new and more effective human resource policy ultimately emerges.

From a policy point of view, it is important to know whether geographical location plays a significant role in the development of human resource policies. It is possible that human resource policies may differ markedly between rural and urban areas, and that institutions in rural areas are not sufficiently profitable to carry the predominantly short-term costs involved in adopting affirmative action programmes. Equally, managers and workers in rural areas may be unaware of the (net) benefits to be had from affirmative action policies, and may therefore be less inclined than their urban counterparts to adopt such policies.

A decision to implement affirmative action programmes may result from increased pressure exerted by organised labour, or from influence brought to bear by politicians, government officials and representatives of multinational companies. It is therefore possible that the extent and nature of affirmative action programmes may vary in accordance with the degree of organisation of the work-force and its ability to exert pressure on management, and also with the extent to which managers are exposed to government officials and other important "third parties". Such variation is bound to cut across different sectors and industries within a particular geographical location, and across different locations within a particular sector or industry.

Conclusion

There are a variety of reasons why institutions in the private and public sectors have recently begun to practise affirmative action. Some employers may be doing so out of a sense of social responsibility or to boost their reputation, while others may view affirmative action as simply another name for the practice of appointing the "best person for the institution". In such cases, companies consider the so-called "reaction qualifications" of potential candidates, or their ability to evoke positive reactions from "third parties", in an attempt to maximise the net benefit of such appointments.

The ability of a firm to implement an affirmative action programme depends on a complex range of social and economic factors, including both cyclical and structural economic changes, geographical location of the firm and its exposure to outside influences. The relative importance of these factors is bound to vary with the type of sector, industry and individual firm, and it therefore seems unwise even to consider imposing a uniform policy of racial and gender quotas. Such a policy would have a patently discriminatory effect on the economy and would thus be difficult to justify on either efficiency or equity grounds. The alternative of a more selective application of quotas is likely to face severe data constraints and involve inordinately high administration costs.

Our tentative conclusion is that the introduction of a quota system could undermine the allocation and distribution of resources in the economy, or prove to be too costly to administer. Moreover, its impact on the racial and gender composition of the labour force could well be limited. ▲

Endnotes

1. This study was made possible by the award of the Fred du Plessis Research Bursary. The authors would like to thank Sanlam for its financial support.

References

Akerlof, GA (1976) "The Economics of Caste and of the Rat Race, and Other Woeful Tales", in *Quarterly Journal of Economics*, Vol 90.

Akerlof, GA (1980) "A Theory of Social Custom, of which Unemployment may be One Consequence", in *Quarterly Journal of Economics*, Vol 94.

Black, PA (1993) "Affirmative Action: Rational Response to a Changing Environment", in *South African Journal of Economics*, Vol 61.

Black, PA (1995) "Affirmative Action in South Africa, or Rational Discrimination a la Akerlof", mimeo, University of Cape Town.

Kemp, N (1993) "Affirmative Action: Legal Obligation or Prudent Business?" in *Human Resources Magazine*, Vol 5.

Madi, PM (1993) *Affirmative Action in Corporate South Africa: Surviving in the Jungle* (Cape Town: Juta).

Maphai, VT (1989) "Affirmative Action in South Africa: A Genuine Option?" in *Social Dynamics*, Vol 15.

O'Regan, C and C Thompson (1993) "Equality for Women in Employment: Collective Bargaining and the Promotion of Equality", unpublished paper, University of Cape Town.

Patel, E (1993) "Economic Empowerment: A Trade Union View", in D Innes, et al (eds), *Reversing Discrimination: Affirmative Action in the Workplace* (Cape Town: Oxford University Press).

Roodt, A (1992) "Black Advancement: Personal and Corporate Responsibility", in *Human Resources Magazine*, Vol 8.

Chapter 13

Treading the thorny path to equity

Mamphela Ramphele

Director, Public Information Centre
Institute for Democracy in South Africa
Vice-Chancellor
University of Cape Town

The cruel reality of the legacy of disadvantage is a challenge which political leaders have to face squarely, instead of creating unrealistic expectations among ordinary people. Creative management of the transition to a better future for the next generation would be the best measure of good leadership.

Introduction

A lot of heat is generated by the affirmative action (AA) debate in South Africa but little light seems to emerge from the process. Affirmative action is a hotly contested concept globally and South Africa cannot escape such contestation. This paper aims to examine the current discourse around the concept and to identify some of the key areas of contestation. Some of the confounding and confusing issues which seem to muddy the waters are identified, and alternative formulations are suggested for the type of corrective action needed to redress aspects of the legacy of the past. Such corrective action is not only inevitable but also imperative for South Africa if our newfound democracy is to have any real meaning and substance for ordinary citizens.

The adoption of the Reconstruction and Development Programme (RDP) by the government of national unity is a symbolic statement which acknowledges the need for a national process of righting the wrongs of the past. The Afrikaans expression *regstellende aksie* (literally, corrective action) captures the essence of what is at the heart of affirmative action in the eyes of those committed to it.

For those feeling threatened by its implications for their own positions and the opportunities that they fear may be closed to them, affirmative action represents a retrogressive step for a country emerging from a state of division between those privileged by virtue of the colour of their skin, on the one hand, and those systematically deprived of opportunities by the apartheid system, on the other.

But among those expressing misgivings about AA are also well-meaning South Africans who are anxious to avoid replacing one wrong with another. Is there a way out of this bind?

The concept

There are a number of obstacles to clarity in the debate on affirmative action. There seem to be as many interpretations of the term as there are interpreters. For some it means turning the tables. "It is now our turn!" seems to be the rallying cry from some people who have been disadvantaged by apartheid. Such an interpretation burdens affirmative action with connotations of punitive action against those previously advantaged. It is also an interpretation which tends to evoke the strongest emotions from both sides of the divide.

At the opposite end of the spectrum from the advocates of this simplistic "table turning" approach are the die-hards, who refuse to acknowledge that there was any systematic discrimination against segments of the South African population under apartheid. They feel that they have acquired resources differentially simply because they were more enterprising than others and thus deserving of the material rewards they have accumulated. A novel version of this view is the assertion by Foreign Affairs Director-General Rusty Evans that the charge that his department was dominated by white males was unfair, since he and his peers should not be held responsible for the "accident of their birth" as white males!

Somewhat more nuanced and more widely held is the view that some people have been disadvantaged by the legacy of apartheid and should thus be first in the queue for resources, whatever their personal circumstances might be. This is the dominant position within the Black Management Forum (BMF), which argues for the empowerment of blacks in the business world from which they were systematically excluded by apartheid, and proposes a quota system as a solution. This view is criticised by those analysts who are troubled by the lack of gender sensitivity within the BMF and its tendency to equate black men with black people in general.

Colour coding is a further confounding variable in the interpretation of affirmative action. For the majority of vocal advocates of affirmative action, the colour question is paramount and has to be incorporated into any policy aimed at undoing the colour-coded apartheid legacy.

The 1993 poverty survey undertaken by the World Bank and the South African Labour Development Research Unit (Saldru) is among the sources of data supporting the contention that poverty in South Africa has a definite colour dimension: 95 percent of South Africa's poor are African, five percent are coloured and less than one percent Indian. It is therefore logical that Africans should be the major beneficiaries of any corrective action.

But advocates of colour-coded AA often fail to point out that poverty in South Africa also has strong geographical, gender and age dimensions. For example, 75 percent of impoverished South Africans are concentrated in the former "independent homelands" of Transkei, Bophuthatswana, Venda and Ciskei, while poverty rates are 50 percent higher in female-headed households. Moreover, some 61 percent of South African children live in poverty.

These statistics notwithstanding, the most vocal advocates of affirmative action are rarely women or people who are rurally based or child-focused. Colour-coded affirmative action policies which do not take additional differentials of power into account are bound to be limited in their purported aim of redressing past inequities.

The Western Cape is a particularly difficult region to deal with in relation to affirmative action, given the legacy of the Coloured Labour Preference Policy which denied many Africans education and training as well as job opportunities. Poverty has a strong employment dimension in South Africa: unemployment among the poor stands at 50 percent and Africans suffer unemployment rates that are nearly twice those of coloureds (38 percent and 21 percent respectively), and nearly 10 times the rate among whites (four percent nationally).

That there is a case for *regstellende aksie* seems to be accepted by all, but who should be the beneficiaries? Strong feelings are emerging among segments of the population previously classified as coloured that they stand to lose from the colour-coded AA approach because they are seen by some public policy makers, and implementers in both the public and the private sector, as not being black enough.

The struggle for power between the ANC and the National Party (NP) in the Western Cape also confounds the issue. The NP is quick to point to the dangers that the ANC's affirmative action policies pose to the position of coloureds – a new form of *swart gevaar* (danger posed by blacks). These charges have not been adequately dealt with by the ANC leadership, either regionally or nationally, perhaps because of the apparent lack of clarity on the part of the leadership about the implications of AA and its management in a complex environment such as the Western Cape.

Rank and file interpretations go unchallenged and bedevil social relations at all levels: in the living environment, involving housing and schooling; in the workplace and in trade union dynamics; in youth organisations and so on. Given its past record, the NP can hardly claim to be a credible advocate of the development of poor coloured people. However, it seems to be getting away with its *swart gevaar* tactics in the absence of a clear response from the ANC to the genuine fear of ordinary coloured people.

Key considerations

There are key issues which need to be taken on board in the debate on AA if we are to move beyond either importing unworkable public policies or continuing to wander in a policy vacuum which breeds its own anxieties. First, it is important to acknowledge the need to redress the distortions which apartheid has bequeathed to our society. A casual examination of national statistics leaves one with a distinct sense of missed opportunities.

Our human resource base is distorted in favour of white males, who constitute a minority of a minority, thus denying the country the wide base of skills essential for accelerated economic growth in an increasingly competitive global environment. The 1992 National Manpower Commission report estimated that, if a growth rate of three percent per annum is to be attained and maintained, the country will be short of 288 000 high-level person-power units – a serious developmental constraint by any measure.

The high levels of income disparities in South Africa will continue to be a source of conflict in the workplace. Workers charge that it is iniquitous for management, paid on the basis of First World standards, to expect workers on the shop floor to accept wages based on Third World standards. Indeed, the level of inequality in South Africa, as measured by the Gini coefficient of 0,61, is second only to Brazil's 0,63.

These inequities are reflected in various ways. For example, the 1993 World Bank/Saldru poverty survey found that the 40 percent of South African households at the lowest end of the poverty spectrum – making up 53 percent of the population – accounted for less than 10 percent of the total national consumption in 1993. By contrast, the 10 percent who constitute the most wealthy households, making up only 5,8 percent of the population, accounted for 40 percent of consumption.

The conspicuous nature of this consumption – in the form of luxury cars, palatial houses and holiday homes – generates enormous anger and frustration among the majority of poor people. They feel that their poverty has been systematically generated by political designs and rightly demand that it should be redressed through an equally deliberate political programme.

The second key consideration is that it is vital to situate the debate about AA within an equity framework. The emphasis should be on access to opportunities, personal development of all people at an institutional level, and changing the institutional culture to reflect a greater diversity of experience and orientation, so that all participants feel at home in a given setting. AA within such an equity framework would be properly located as a strategy to achieve set goals, rather than constituting an end in itself.

An equity framework would have a number of qualitative benefits.

- It would create a sound moral or ethical basis for national policy, rather than a punitive one, acknowledging that part of the definition of full citizenship is the right to make demands on the state to create an environment in which basic needs can be met.
- It would enable one to address differentials of power both between and within various segments of South African society which have been affected by apartheid in qualitatively different ways, for example, rural women and children versus women and children elsewhere, black women versus white women, poor uneducated men versus successful black male businesspeople, and coloured people versus Africans in relation to such issues as access to housing or land in the Western Cape. Failure to focus on these differentials will lead to entrenchment of existing inequities and greater frustration.
- It would enable one to develop a "win-win" scenario at an institutional level, with all participants benefiting from the process of change towards a more person-orientated management and leadership approach. In such a "win-win" scenario, those who were the beneficiaries of apartheid and have higher skill levels as a result would be more likely to participate in the empowerment of, and support for, those needing to develop their full potential. Resentful

middle and senior management can sabotage the most carefully crafted staff development process.

- Finally, it would enable one to tackle institutional cultural questions which often get buried in anger and resentment, but also get used as an excuse for non-performance. The dominance of Anglo-Saxon culture in most major national institutions, coupled with demands for the use of English as the lingua franca, poses enormous obstacles to the harmonisation of relations between various sections of the population. Opening a discussion around the issue of institutional culture and laying bare that which is often silently interred in habit, could go a long way to improving the climate of many institutions in our society.

Third, it is crucial to acknowledge that AA cannot be a panacea for all past wrongs. There are limitations to the extent to which one can correct past wrongs – one may have to make peace with the past. For example, those excluded from educational opportunities over the past five decades cannot hope to be put in the position they might otherwise have enjoyed; nor can one do much about those educationally disadvantaged over the last decade or two, beyond remedial education.

The cruel reality of the legacy of disadvantage is a challenge which political leaders have to face squarely instead of creating unrealistic expectations among ordinary people. Creative management of the transition to a better future for the next generation would be the best measure of good leadership.

Fourth, AA has to be targeted carefully if it is to succeed. AA has to create the environment for success but cannot guarantee personal success. Society has an obligation to create an affirming environment but the individual has to take responsibility to make every effort to succeed. Failure to locate responsibility where it appropriately belongs often contributes to frustration, guilt and anger on all sides.

But can AA work in all areas of disadvantage which are part of the legacy of the past? Should one have AA in basic service provision, such as health, education, housing, transport and so on? What would be the consequences of a national AA programme for the provision of these material resources for the country as a whole? Would it be feasible and sustainable?

The ANC, as the major partner in the government of national unity, finds itself in the difficult position of having to try to live up to its election promise to provide 200 000 houses a year over five years to wipe out the backlog. It is difficult for the ANC to justify the discrepancy between the housing policy of the apartheid government for poor white, Indian and coloured people, which provided houses for both subsidised rental and ownership, and the incremental approach of the current policy directed at the large number of poor African households.

The reality is that, while it was fairly easy to provide for a small proportion of the population by denying the needs of the majority, the South African fiscus of the 1990s will simply not be able to shoulder the burden of a four-roomed house for all unhoused people. It would be a recipe for national bankruptcy. Hard decisions have to be taken.

What about the place of "black economic empowerment" in the AA debate? Does the creation of opportunities for a few blacks at the top of the economic scale constitute "black empowerment"? There is no doubt that part of the legacy of apartheid is the concentration of wealth in the hands of a few, mainly white males. The 1991 census suggests that 75 percent of those earning annual incomes of R300 000 or more were white males, while only four percent were African women. By contrast, only four percent of white males reported that they had no source of income, compared to 42 percent of African women.

Does "black empowerment" address the race and gender nature of wealth accumulation? Current evidence points to a tendency for black men to join white males in wealth accumulation and ownership of the means of production. But is that in itself a desirable tendency?

I personally see no difficulty in people enriching themselves, provided two conditions are met. The first is that personal enrichment should not be confused with black empowerment: one cannot be fabulously rich on behalf of others. An assertion to the contrary would be taking collective identity politics too far.

The second condition is that those asserting that their ownership of the means of production is part of black empowerment should have to demonstrate that this is in fact the case. For example, in what way do black-owned enterprises differ from others in their management of employees and their investment in the personal development of staff, and how enabling is the institutional culture of such establishments? There is no evidence thus far that these questions form a central part of the AA debate in our society.

Fifth, AA has to have clear goals and a time horizon. There has to be an understanding that AA programmes can run for only five, 10 or 15 years. No society can sustain indefinite AA programmes without creating permanent cleavages between citizens. Time scales are important for both the beneficiaries of AA and those who have to support them. It would help to concentrate the mind if people knew that they had to maximise their efforts before the special window of opportunity closed. It should not be acceptable for one who had access to quality higher education and job opportunities in the 1990s to argue in 10 years' time that he/she was disadvantaged by apartheid, and therefore deserves a special dispensation.

Some disadvantages will be easier to overcome than others, and a staggered schedule for phasing out AA would therefore be necessary. But there has to be light at the end of the tunnel, not least because of the symbolic significance of expressing confidence in a future beyond historical divisions.

Set targets and goals often raise alarm about quotas and it is therefore important to distinguish between goals and quotas. Quotas are prescriptive and restrictive frameworks which leave little room for initiative on the part of institutional actors. Goals set over a time horizon are like a budget, which sets a framework for action and enables one to compare performance against commitments.

Such goals should be set realistically in the light of available resources, both material and human, if they are to be seen as achievable. For example, however much one may be committed to AA, it would be unrealistic to expect current race and gender imbalances in tertiary educational institutions to be eliminated within five years. Some 95 percent of all South African professors are currently white males and it will take at least a decade to change this, given the spread of higher educational qualifications, the time it takes to move up the career ladder in some of the highly technical areas, and the low turnover of academic staff.

Failure to take cognisance of such realities would lead to frustration for all involved. At the same time, however, it cannot be argued convincingly that access to education and training, as well as to lower- and middle-level jobs, should be delayed for any length of time.

Some tough questions

It is important to acknowledge that, however meticulously one might formulate an AA policy within an equity framework, the very fact of having to distinguish between categories of people generates tensions. Consequently, there are a number of tough questions that need to be faced squarely.

First, in what way are those citizens who deserve AA going to be distinguished from the rest, given the demise of the legislated population classification which was the foundation stone of apartheid? Should policy makers rely on self-classification or devise other means? If the latter, what other means would be appropriate?

Any thought of continuing voluntary race-based birth registration should be evaluated carefully lest future generations be condemned to the folly of the past. The approach in the United States, where "racial categories" are almost set in stone and are proliferating, is not one to be emulated. There is a real danger in such a system of entrenching vested interests by perpetuating differential access to resources, so undermining future harmonious relations in society. It is often the case that the enterprising members of designated groups, who know how to "work the system", end up benefiting more than the most needy members.

The idea of a rainbow nation set in stone and underpinning the continued categorisation of members of a given society is not as attractive as some of its advocates would have us believe. The rainbow metaphor is useful only as an interim measure which acknowledges the diverse and, in some ways, parallel nature of the cultures of the current South African society. However, one hopes that the rainbow is also a symbol of hope that the clouds are lifting.

A rainbow, by definition, encapsulates transition from cloud and rain to sunshine, and is thus a transient phenomenon. One cannot have a rainbow nation as a vision of the future: bright enough sunshine should make possible a blending of different colours into light, with individual colours present but not obtrusive.

If we maintain a focus on equity, socio-economic disadvantage will become the greatest marker of eligibility for AA interventions. To the extent that such measures overtake race-based criteria, to that extent will geographic and socio-economic variables become more reliable measures of disadvantage and thus a more rational basis for public policy intervention. Such an approach should replace the current tendency toward colour-coded AA interventions, which breed a "blacker-than-thou" mentality with all its divisive dangers.

Second, not everybody who stands to benefit from AA is necessarily comfortable with taking the risk of being labelled an "affirmative action" candidate. The more disadvantaged one is, the more vulnerable one may feel to such "labelling", underwritten as it is by the group mentality which is perpetuated by categorising people. One consequence is that people's successes and failures tend to be ascribed to "the group to which they belong", rather than being seen as a measure of individual talent and performance. Existing prejudices tend to be reinforced under such conditions.

Apprehension around the risk of labelling is often heightened by a system in which individuals are promoted beyond their level of competence. The result often is that their poor performance is ascribed to their "group identity", rather than being seen as an indicator of either inadequate institutional support for personal development or lack of potential in the individual to perform beyond a given level.

A third, and related, issue is the risk of a blanket identification of members of particular groups as potential AA candidates and therefore in need of affirmation and training. One has often heard personal narratives of frustrated young blacks and women who have to battle for recognition as accomplished professional people, instead of being seen and treated as trainees in need of support. A hesitancy to give such people real jobs with real responsibilities, because of a fear of the risks they are seen to represent, bedevils institutional relations.

At the same time, one cannot overlook the problem of a small number of blacks and women who hesitate to admit to inadequacies in an environment in which they feel vulnerable. However, such problems can be obviated by a policy of institution-wide, yet individually tailored, entry level interviews aimed at mapping out career paths, identifying strengths and weaknesses, and agreeing on a personal development and training strategy. Regular evaluation of how individuals are doing in relation to their own and institutional goals is an essential part of an affirming work environment.

Fourth, a focus on AA runs the risk of charges of racism or sexism from both sides of the divide. New entrants may experience a backlash from those feeling excluded from opportunities, a situation that brings out the worst in people as a result of the vulnerabilities and anxieties about the future that lie at the heart of such reactions.

Equally possible are charges of racism or sexism from people who fail to perform for reasons unrelated to the institutional environment in which they find themselves. Under such circumstances, accusations of racism or sexism become defences against facing up to personal inadequacies. Creative management of this type of tension is essential to the success of AA programmes.

Fifth, it is important to remember that AA is not a neutral instrument which can be pressed into service for redressing the wrongs of the past. We have had a history of AA in South Africa which eliminated poverty among poor whites at the expense of black people. The First Carnegie Enquiry into Poverty formed the basis for further discrimination against black people: the entrenchment of job reservation denied them access to jobs; differential housing policies favouring poor whites denied them access to houses; and allocation of public resources to poor white children denied them access to education.

One could argue convincingly that apartheid was a massive AA programme for white people and that it specifically targeted white males for additional support to place them in the dominant position they are in today. It is therefore important not to be simplistic in the advocacy of AA, as if it were an inherently good public policy instrument. It has to be used with care, if the creation of further inequities is to be minimised.

Finally, as has been the case in the United States, AA programmes always run the risk of being challenged in a constitutional court on the basis that they violate the rights of categories of individuals who feel excluded from access to opportunities. The interim South African Constitution makes provision for AA programmes and thus minimises the risk of such challenges.

But for how long can an AA approach be sustained without being challenged in individual cases where relative disadvantage may be difficult to prove? For example, a poor white South African denied access to a place and/or financial aid at a tertiary level educational institution while an upper-class black compatriot gained a place and/or financial aid might justifiably claim to be the victim of unfair discrimination.

Conclusion

AA is a strategy which has no inherent moral or ethical basis. Such a basis has to be created by locating AA within a well-thought-out and articulated equity framework. The aim must be to ensure that the greatest good is achieved for the largest number of South Africa's citizens, and that the benefits of such an AA programme do not flow along the contours of existing privilege but address the needs of the most disadvantaged members of our society.

We need to tread carefully on this thorny path. There will be many dangers and pressures for either hasty action or complacency, both of which are the enemies of a more prosperous future for South Africa. We have to keep our eye on the vision of a more equitable democratic society. ▲

Section 5

Non-Racialism

Chapter 14

A politically incorrect view of non-racialism and majority rule

Hermann Giliomee
Professor of Political Studies
University of Cape Town

Imperialistic non-racialism fosters and conceals the African demand for power and control of the widest range of political and social institutions. It is at the same time a rejection of any mobilisation by ethnic minorities or communities to advance their own ethnic or communal claims and interests.

One term, many meanings

Over the past five years, the term "non-racialism" has been the topic of as much intense discussion in South Africa as was "apartheid" between 1943, when the term was first used in parliament, and 1948, when the National Party (NP) came to power. In both cases politicians have given different and sometimes conflicting definitions of the concepts. Like respondents to a Rorsach test, people read into the terms whatever they wish to read. Writer Alan Paton once remarked that apartheid made it possible for the Afrikaner racist and the Afrikaner idealist to believe in the same policy. Something similar may be true of non-racialism.

Late in my career, exasperation about the woolliness of the concept of apartheid compelled me to try to understand its diverse meanings. As far as I know, no one has yet dissected the many meanings of non-racialism. While there is certainly room for a doctoral dissertation on the subject, I would like to simply give an account of the different uses I have encountered.

Three senses

Non-racialism seems to have three meanings. The first boils down to a rejection of all racism or apartheid. It says: "Let's rebuild this country together." It is also a celebration of all cultures, of the diversity in South African society. It is a recognition of people simply as people, of individuals simply as individuals. It is the welcoming of all into the house of Africa, the breaking down of social walls and the expurgation of the pathologies of apartheid. It is World Cup non-racialism; it is rainbow nation non-racialism.[1]

Non-racialism also has two predominantly political meanings. One is a rejection of white supremacy and, more particularly, its attempt at "multi-racial" constitutional engineering. Invariably the colonial powers to the north and white politicians in South Africa used "multi-racial" constitutions to keep blacks separate, divided and out of the mainstream of power.

Colin Legum, a journalist with extensive first-hand experience in covering African politics, gives this account of the origins of the term "non-racialism" in a letter to me in 1993:

> [To] my knowledge, it began to assume political acceptance in the 1950s when British colonial policy was advocating "multi-racial" constitutions for Africa. At the time their model was the successful "multi-racial" constitution of Malaysia. The Colonial Office was using this in particular to justify Sir Edward Twining's proposal for a 10-10-10 allocation of seats to Africans, whites and Indians in Tanganyika. It was then that Julius Nyerere, while still studying in Edinburgh, denounced the idea of "multi-racialism" and in an article, I think, written for the Fabians, employed the idea of "non-racialism". This took root among anti-colonial campaigners.

The term was also used in the 1950s by white communists close to the ANC and by intellectuals in the Non-European Unity Movement. This form of non-racialism, which is in effect a rejection of racial quotas, does not pose any particular difficulty.

But there is another meaning of the term, one which is problematic because it is essentially a form of political and social imperialism. I would like to call this the imperialistic meaning of non-racialism.

Imperialistic non-racialism

Imperialistic non-racialism fosters and conceals the African demand for power and control of the widest range of political and social institutions. It is at the same time a rejection of any mobilisation by ethnic minorities or communities to advance their own ethnic or communal claims and interests. It is Jacobin in that it is prepared to use state resources, particularly in the fields of education, communications and language policy, to weaken ethnic or communal affiliations in order to create space for the new non-racial (read African-led, non-ethnic) nation to be born.

This non-racial project represents a drive which can be threatening to minorities. In a zero-sum way, it aims at displacing minorities from positions of power and blocking their efforts to retain some cultural autonomy.

Non-racialism, as used by its African National Congress (ANC) proponents, is not something that could be interpreted or judged by objective criteria. For instance, there are immediate objections if the NP claims to be the most non-racial party in view of the fact that it has the largest cross-ethnic voter support. For the ANC, one's non-racialism is, above all, judged by one's historical involvement or non-involvement in the black struggle for liberation.

Herein lies a certain amount of irony: the ANC, as the party most strongly espousing non-racialism, is in fact a racial party, depending on Africans for 94 percent of its support. While this may not be the case in the ranks of ANC leadership, most of the non-Africans in ANC leadership positions cannot be said to represent in any significant way their respective communities. They are either people who have actively participated in the struggle or who are co-optees. Nevertheless, in terms of imperialistic non-racialism, the ANC is the "natural ruling party" to use the term coined by ANC minister Kader Asmal.

A further irony is that affirmative action as a policy pursued by the ANC will continue to racialise our society. The African middle class put in place by way of affirmative action has everything to gain by maintaining racial boundaries and a racially structured system of promotion. In view of our history these responses are understandable. What is less understandable is how all of this can be called non-racialism. Do we not have here the counterpart of the sordid habit of apartheid – to call things the exact opposite of what you mean to achieve?

The coloured vote

It is early days and the ANC has yet to spell out its affirmative action policy. No one could object to a policy of equality of opportunity which helps people to compete on level terms. The problem lies with affirmative action which demands equality of outcome. Here we have the rejection of competition, the imposition of quotas and the demand that bodies and institutions must reflect the population composition. Regardless of the assurances ANC leaders may give, this type of affirmative action offers no joy to coloured people for it is in essence an African preferential policy.

This fear of being displaced and of standing last in the row for jobs was a strong incentive for coloured people to vote as they did in the 1994 election. Although the position of coloured people in the 1970s and 1980s has yet to be fully documented, it is clear that they made major social and economic advances during these years under NP rule.[2] Far from being a sham, the tricameral parliament for whites, coloured people and Indians built a significant number of houses and schools and improved pensions for these groups – and for coloured people in particular.

Infant mortality rates and life expectancy are among the best indicators we have of the social welfare of a community. According to these criteria the coloured community made considerable headway during the apartheid years. American demographer Nicholas Eberstadt (1995: 160 – 161) reports that coloured male life expectancy increased by nine years between 1950 and 1985 while that of females jumped a full 15 years. Between 1970 and 1985 the coloured infant mortality rate dropped by more than two thirds. Eberstadt comments: "Hardly any population on record has to date enjoyed such a rapid and sustained pace of improvement in child survival. Though unheralded in South Africa, it represents a major achievement in public health".

Eberstadt ascribes the improvement to "an increase in the availability and quality of government services (including health care) extended to the coloured population over these years".

So I do not agree with some participants who said the NP never cared for the poor other than the white poor. Attending some NP meetings in coloured townships in the 1994 election campaign, I did not get the impression of a poor community that had been left behind as a result of apartheid. Instead, the main impression I got was of a community fearing to lose the gains they had made in the previous decade or so.

Why did two-thirds of the coloured people in the Western Cape vote NP in April 1994? Was it a class- or identity-oriented vote? In elections, although people bear their particular economic and class concerns in mind, they usually look through an ethnic or community prism when choosing a party to advance these interests. Voting is also a way of designating one's political affiliation and the place of one's group in society. Perhaps the clearest example of that is the voting behaviour of the Afrikaners in the 1960s and 1970s.

This does not mean that the vote is simply there to be collected, regardless of a party's candidates, policy platform or past record. As explained above, the NP did, to some extent, deliver with respect to the coloured people under the tricameral system. In the 1994 election, the NP managed to persuade most coloured people in the Western Cape that it was on their side. If coloured people had not made progress relative to Africans the NP, with its apartheid albatross, would have enjoyed little success. In this sense, then, one can use the term "racial census" for the outcome of the 1994 election: the choice of political party correlated with the position in the racial or ethnic hierarchy of a particular group. Of course, there were also those coloured people – mostly the well-educated – who felt most strongly about the way the NP had discriminated against them and humiliated them. They tended to vote strongly ANC.

Options

Coloured people must chose between three options. The first is the separatism of the Kleurling Weerstandsbeweging, which to my mind has no viability. The second is to mobilise with the aim of taking over groups such as the Western Cape NP or ANC. I doubt that this will be successful for the simple reason that the high degree of centralism in the South African government forces people to think nationally and to choose national, rather than provincial, political vehicles. National parties are compelled to become maximal coalitions incorporating different classes and ethnic groups. In such coalitions, politicians talk vaguely in terms of values and aspirations and avoid sectionalist messages. Both leaders and followers believe that to engage in sectional talk is to concede that the party is unable to transcend its narrow (ethnic) bounds and is therefore weak. For this reason there are limits to the "coloured-isation" of the NP or ANC in the Western Cape.

This is not to deny that there is considerable scope for a sharp increase in coloured representatives and leadership within the main parties. However, it is unclear how this could be achieved in the case of the Western Cape ANC, given the recent tensions in this organisation.

In the case of the NP, the most promising route may be to redefine the concept of Afrikaner inclusively. NP politician Peter Marais is on solid historical ground when he calls himself an Afrikaner. In the 18th, 19th and early 20th centuries the term was used for people of both "European" and "mixed" descent. It was only between 1950 and 1980, when an exclusive Afrikaner nationalism exerted ideological hegemony, that the term "Afrikaner" was used exclusively for white Afrikaans-speakers. That hegemony is now broken forever and I welcome the rise of "Afrikaner" as a non-racial term for anyone who values Afrikaans.

The third option is to rely on the Constitution to protect identities and interests. I tend to be sceptical about the protection offered by the Constitution except in the case of certain first generation rights. The strong African demand for redistribution and affirmative action is likely to prevail over both the Constitution and the efforts of politicians to extend affirmative action to coloured people.

Those who have drawn up the interim Constitution like to assure us that, by protecting individual rights, the identity and interests of the group or community to which a person belongs is also protected. The University of the Western Cape (UWC) offers a good example of the fallacy of this argument. In pursuit of the ANC ideal of nation building, the medium of instruction at UWC and the composition of its student body – and with that the very identity of the institution – were fundamentally altered without a single individual right being violated. Moreover, this was done without consulting the community.

Paradox posed by Westminster

Much is being said currently about nation building, reconciliation and co-operation. Yet the paradox is that South Africa's final Constitution will almost certainly see a return to the Westminster system which, other than the past 15 months, has held sway throughout South African history.

According to the Westminster system, the executive and legislative branches of government are fused and full control of government rests with the party which wins the general election. This model confers enormous power on the victorious party – hence the saying "the winner takes all" as a description of the system. The winner invariably employs power to erode the autonomy of institutions such as the central bank and universities, as was done by the NP when it was in power.

Those in the opposition must not fool themselves into believing that the overwhelming majority support of the ANC is temporary. Comparative analyses show that in deeply divided societies such as South Africa, electoral alliances will be built on race or ethnicity and they will be stable. Under Westminster, there will be clear winners and losers who will become permanent winners and permanent losers. Moreover, the winners and losers will have a distinctive racial and ethnic character.

As a result, Westminster produces conflict – in fact it the most conflictual democratic system that exists. This is why it has been discredited as a system and why no new democracy has accepted it in the past 20 years. Instead, new democracies have tried to limit the power of the majority party and to encourage coalition building. It is a huge irony that the ANC, which prides itself on its progressive character, is the party that is taking us back to Westminster.

The ANC believes that it will gain greater power to transform society by terminating the government of national unity and returning to Westminster. But the chances are that simple majority rule will confer less power and authority because the victorious racial group will be confronted by resentful minorities. One may see tax revolts and rent and service charge boycotts in non-African communities. It is for this reason that the ANC may be willing to enter into a voluntary coalition after the election of 1999.

But without any kind of "coalition policy accord", this may be a hollow gesture. Perhaps what people who see themselves as part of the opposition may do is to start thinking at an early stage about the type of policy accord they want and to hold their respective parties to mandates on a policy accord. However, there is little hope of this taking place because political power lies with the party that can determine the agenda. For the foreseeable future, the ANC will be able to do just that. ▲

Endnote

1. "World Cup non-racialism" refers to the symbolic nation building espoused at the opening and closing ceremonies of the 1995 Rugby World Cup and the surge of identification and pride across ethnic lines following the South African team's victories.

2. M McGrath and A Whitehead argue that between 1975 and 1991, the income of the top 60 percent of coloured people increased by a fifth, while the lowest 40 percent decreased by about five percent. By contrast, the income of the lowest 40 percent of Africans decreased by 40 percent.

References

1. Eberstadt, N (1995) *The Tyranny of Numbers: Mismeasurement and Misrule* (Washington: AEI Press).

2. McGrath M and A Whitehead (1994) "Disparate Circumstances", in *Indicator*, Vol 11, No 3.

Chapter 15

Cultural diversity and national unity

Barbara Masekela
South African Ambassador to France

When I was a child, the Cape Province, Natal and the North-

ern Province were faraway places with exotic inhabitants.

Muslim, Pedi and Zulu women were fascinating and mys-

terious characters but, when they came to live in Witbank,

they became auntie and "ousie" and "ouma".

The meaning of non-racialism in South Africa must be viewed against the background of the historical record of our country. It is crucial, before we rush to judgement, that we understand the objective reality of the economic, social and political legacy inherited by the present government. The extent of the progress made by the ANC-led democratic government in its very short period of power should be measured in relation to the concrete conditions of our heritage.

In principle, therefore, to make a fair assessment we must take into account such factors as the provincial borders. Why were they drawn in the first place and by whom? How did industrial and agricultural development impinge on the economic well-being of those communities? What are the communication systems? Are they effective? What are the social and cultural facilities available and how are they distributed? What kind of financial allocations were rendered to them by previous governments?

We are compelled also to acknowledge that our multi-cultural society is made up of components whose attitudes and mores have been shaped by the interests of imperialist powers, coloni-alism and apartheid ideology. All were characterised by the use of ethnicity to maintain control and to derive optimum economic exploitation, whether for the mother country or for dominant minority groups settled within South Africa.

Thus it is that we are confronted time and time again by our own mixed responses. For exam-ple, we recognise and even admire the spirit that informed the struggle against British colonial-ism during the Boer War, but we recoil from and condemn the subsequent relentless assaults upon the human rights of black South Africans. We agitate for the rights of minorities, but who speaks loudly enough of the Khoi and the San people?

The achievement of national unity in a multi-cultural society is a process that evolves over generations. Ingrained attitudes do not disappear magically or overnight. Nevertheless, good legislation and the goodwill of active community participation can help to accelerate transforma-tion.

Current events in Bosnia and Rwanda highlight for us the importance of creating new institu-tions that go beyond the self-interest of opportunist groups who refuse to consider the interde-pendence of all the components of our multi-cultural society. What is at stake is our very sur-vival.

Indeed, we are not all the same in every way and we do not have everything in common. What we do have in common is that we are human beings, equal under the law, and all burdened by a deeply embedded racism that continues to threaten our nationhood.

In our new democratic order, some of us are capitalising on the democratic right to dissent and new pockets of ultra-militancy are emerging from the most unexpected quarters. This is a measure of the achievement of democratic governance in South Africa: our people have attained freedom of expression and they are using it.

The emergence of a Coloured Resistance Movement in the Western Cape is therefore not surprising. However, the complexity of the debate around coloured identity should not be under-estimated.

True stories

Those of us who were raised in mixed communities, before the strict ethnic divisions of apartheid were imposed, had the benefit of all the South African worlds. We lived cheek by jowl with Indian, Chinese and coloured people and our grandmothers told us stories of how poor white mothers, barefoot and ragged, would come begging for food at their villages before we were born. Our teachers set aside the history textbooks and told us the true stories of the determined resist-ance of African people.

In the coal-mining town of Witbank, we played with Ndebele, Swazi, Mozambican, Venda and Xhosa children and sometimes, on special occasions, their mothers wore colourful national cos-tumes and were bedecked with beads. We were not threatened. Yes, our coloured relatives made reference to our *kroes hare* (curly hair) and flat noses and we heard people call our mother a *Boesman* (Bushman), but we did not care because, at the Church of England Primary School, the Xhosa principal always reminded me what a bright student my mother had been. Besides, nobody dared disparage my mother to her face in any language, since she knew them all.

In other words, we were exposed as children to a rich and varied cultural milieu, which broadened our horizons and gave us a fuller than usual view of South African realities. We were not forced into denial.

We cannot recreate the past. But we can revive and apply the good customs that shaped our communities in the past and we can combine them with advocacy of non-sexism, non-racialism and unity. When I was a child, the Cape Province, Natal and the Northern Province were faraway places with exotic inhabitants. Muslim, Pedi and Zulu women were fascinating and mysterious characters but, when they came to live in Witbank, they became auntie and *ousie* (elder sister) and *ouma* (grandmother). I learnt to know them. Later on, my parents sent me to Inanda Girls' Seminary in Natal and I passed Zulu language and literature with flying colours.

All this explains my social background and my political choice. I could not but choose to support non-racialism and unity and, later on, fight for non-sexism.

What I am saying is that, during the era when we were referred to as non-whites and non-Europeans, we were evolving towards an integrated society which nevertheless recognised and respected the richness of our cultural diversity. When, through no fault of our own, fragmentation and ethnicity became the rule, many of us were locked into rural or ethnic compartments with no windows. We need to break down the walls of those compartments so that we can move out of our cultural confinement into the light of the wide South Africa that belongs to us all.

Presently, it is only those with economic mobility who can benefit from the freedom for which we have all made such great sacrifices. Even then, our cultural advancement at this stage is still dictated by what was formerly created for the privileged classes. We run the danger of creating a new elite that is schooled in the values of a white liberal establishment.

A wish list

Effective change requires an active programme that will not compromise in regard to breaking down the barriers of the past. What follows represents a wish list of some of the strategies that we could employ in the enterprise of achieving a non-racial South Africa.

1. Formal education must remain a priority. However, the school curriculum must be overhauled to give our youth an authentic view of our history and culture, and the teaching of the sciences and mathematics should be emphasised. Our children must be equipped with the technical knowledge to enable them to participate fully in the modern world.

2. Informal education must become a feature of our nation. The existing high level of illiteracy calls for an innovative, universal approach to literacy that should employ the skills of all those who can already read and write. Materials and teaching aids should be made available to communities to encourage them to participate directly in a national literacy programme. All our people must be empowered to understand the complex processes of a contemporary government.

3. There should be revision of the allocation of resources so that there is balanced development. Sparsely populated and rural areas must be given the consideration due to their special circumstances.

4. The government must consider a housing policy that does not encourage the maintenance of ethnic neighbourhoods.

5. There should be an agreement on minimum cultural facilities in every community, so that our people can have access to the products of various art forms.
6. The learning of a language other than the mother tongue must be fostered.
7. Attention should be given to the creation of public spaces such as sports grounds and parks.
8. National monuments, museums and the like must be accessible to all and a conscious effort should be made to encourage people to visit them.
9. Public buildings erected for the use of so-called "own affairs" governments must be allocated to appropriate institutions and utilised for the benefit of the people.
10. Racial insults must be punishable by law.
11. We must encourage South Africans to visit other parts of the country through a conscious programme of internal tourism.
12. We must draw from the best of other cultures so that our people gain a broader view of other societies.
13. Traditional South African architectural and democratic techniques should be promoted in tandem with the emulation of modern universal design.
14. New housing plans must include recreational facilities.
15. We must establish a national orchestra, or dance group, or opera company charged with developing a uniquely South African production with an inclusive cultural imperative.

Chapter 16

The Great Gariep: metaphors of national unity in the new South Africa

Neville Alexander

Director
Project for the Study of Alternative Education in South Africa
University of Cape Town

If the nation does not become the primary identity of the people of South Africa, they will imbibe willy-nilly all manner of ethnic and racial allegiances or sub-identities as their ideological life-blood.

Identity

The founding myth of the nation-to-be in the new South Africa is the concept of non-racialism. There are those, like academic Johan Degenaar [1], who believe in all sincerity that we are playing with fire by even suggesting that we are building a nation, since this implies the pernicious notion of a collective consciousness. Instead, they believe, we are on safer ground if we confine ourselves to the complex task of "building democracy". This is certainly not a trivial point of view. The problem with it is that it rests on the assumption that alternative collective identities are less "dangerous" or, indeed, that such identities are avoidable.

The fact is, of course, that group identities are inherent in ideology which is itself a survival mechanism or a comfort zone in which the individual feels secure. We usually think of stereotypes as the images we acquire or create of "the Other". In reality, we do exactly the same thing, but in a narcissistic manner, with images of "Self". In other words, identity is also a stereotype. To put the matter more simply, if the nation does not become the primary identity of the people of South Africa, they will imbibe willy-nilly all manner of ethnic and racial allegiances or subidentities as their ideological life-blood.

Degenaar's view is also weakened by the empirical fact that, in the new South Africa, we *are* building a nation. The very theme of this conference is the most appropriate relationship between an overarching national unity and the diverse sub-identities which the people of this country have taken on or acquired in the course of historic struggles.

Non-racialism

Non-racialism, as an ideological construct, is derived from a class-reductionist, orthodox Marxist paradigm. In its most uncompromising expression, it implies that racial consciousness is a "false" consciousness, since "race" is irrelevant to one's social being. This position becomes even more tenable when it can be shown that "race" is not a valid biological entity, a view that now has the imprimatur of the United Nations Educational, Scientific and Cultural Organisation (Unesco), for what it is worth.

The problem with such a reductionist position is that it equates materiality with social reality, that is, it holds that "reality" is one-dimensional. Today, it is trite to remark that belief in the reality of a phenomenon has the same pertinent effects as if the phenomenon were material. On the other hand, it is important from the point of view of strategy and social intervention to construct an ontological hierarchy of relevant phenomena. One's interventions are bound to have more chance of success if it is clear that one is dealing with belief structures, rather than with infrastructural phenomena such as waning natural assets.

Historically, in the South African context, non-racialism as a political platform goes back to the Communist Party of South Africa. This idea, among many others, was among the most important of the significant civilising contributions of that party to South African society. The development of the idea of non-racialism was a natural reaction of the radical intelligentsia to the racist practices of the colonial overlords and the white supremacists in the Union of South Africa. It was fed by the intense battles waged by Europe's most skilful intellectuals against the Social Darwinist attack on the working class and on black people.

From the 1940s onwards, the idea of non-racialism became associated in the public mind with the Non-European Unity Movement, which conducted a fiery polemic against the Congress movement's multi-racialism at the time and well into the 1960s. The rights and wrongs of that particular period need not detain us here but it should be recorded that, at the public level, it was the Unity Movement more than any other organisation which propagated this platform after World War II. They, together with the radicals in the Congress movement, succeeded in imprinting on the minds of probably most of the young intelligentsia at the liberal universities and at Fort Hare, an understanding of "race" as "humanity's most dangerous myth". In the aftermath of the geno-cidal practices of the Nazis and in the context of the virulent racism of the National Party (NP) in South Africa, this particular lesson was learnt thoroughly.

So thoroughly, in fact, that in the infancy of the social sciences in South Africa, an impercep-tible over-generalisation took place from the reductionist denial of the social reality of "race" to the denial of the existence of all group solidarities. The machiavellian manipulations of the social engineers of the South African Bureau of Racial Affairs (Sabra) and other NP think-tanks con-solidated in the minds of these intellectuals the notion that ethnic solidarities are as artificial as racial identities.

Without going into the detail I have explored in many other essays, it can be said that a historic divide arose between those on the right who adopted the cultural definition of nationality prevalent in the practices and theories of Eastern and Central European social movements, and those located to the left of the spectrum of South African politics who adopted the political defi-nition of nationality implicit in the history and theories of such movements in Western Europe. The former position served to legitimate the segregationist politics of the ruling class under the political motto of the NP, *Ons bou 'n nasie*, ("We build a nation") and acquired its ultimate social form in the apartheid state. It also reinforced the position of the proponents of non-racialism, who rejected as primitive tribalism any notion of ethnic solidarity and insisted that only the nation had any meaningful connection with the modernisation project. This view was underlined in the Unity Movement's epigrammatic injunction: "Let Us Build a Nation!"

The NP, with the resources of political power at its disposal, could give substance to its culturalist design of a multi-national South African state, a project that thankfully has now been abandoned. The deleterious effects of the practices and institutions the NP entrenched are the reason for this conference. The Unity Movement, as well as those in the Congress movement who were not implicitly trapped in a four-nations paradigm, did virtually nothing – other than produc-ing political propaganda – to promote the realisation of their view of a single South African nation.

Although it would not have been easy, it is quite conceivable, for example, that the leadership of that movement could have promoted the learning of African languages among English- and Afrikaans-speaking South Africans.

Equally, they could have facilitated the learning of English and Afrikaans among speakers of African languages, with a view to facilitating communication among all the people. This is but one example of many possible social movements that might have been promoted, as the example of the Afrikaans language movements shows so eloquently. However, the ingrained Anglocentrism of the black middle class in South Africa led the national liberation movement – and the people – into a cul-de-sac as far as language policy is concerned.

In reality, as we can now see very clearly, an initially progressive and radical view of the South African social formation atrophied to become a zone of comfort for middle-class people. Indeed, for many the very idea of a South African nation became problematical, since it was inextricably linked to white South Africa at the time. In the end, a kind of cosmopolitan ambience enveloped this leadership, which became even more out of touch with the state of consciousness of the working class on whom it depended to make the revolution.

On the ground, the "masses" had always accepted in one degree or another the identities described for them in ruling-class ideology. This was, and is, the basis of the ideological class struggle or the battle for the hearts and minds of "the people". In South Africa, then as now, the salient identities thus described were, and are, those of four historically evolved colour castes, and it was folly to fail to acknowledge this and to address its social implications.

The Great Gariep

What was not understood by most of this leadership was the fact that non-racialism did not necessarily imply the denial of the reality of the other social markers around which people create stereotypes of others and of themselves. The material undergirding of the social reality of such stereotypes is always a purely historical matter, that is, subject to contestation by contending social forces.

This, incidentally, is one of the reasons why the reprehensible interpretation of "affirmative action" applied by certain private sector (and public sector) interests in the Western Cape is such an act of folly. Failure to address such seemingly trivial issues will cost us dearly. Neglect of the subtleties of our own history could easily lead us to an unstoppable slide into a Bosnian or even a Rwandan scenario. If KwaZulu-Natal teaches us nothing else, it surely should alert us to the fact that these are not simply empty speculations.

The resurgence of ethnic consciousness after February 1990 and especially after April 1994 is not surprising, given the economic terrain on which the transition to democracy is being negotiated. Both fears and aspirations play a role in this drama, most spectacularly in the "liberal" Western Cape.

It is also clear that identities have never been as fluid in South Africa as they are today. Even a cursory glance at what is happening among Afrikaans-speaking whites demonstrates the truth of this assertion. The same thing is happening among all the people. Most options are open and the reality of multiple identities has become the opportunity of identity planners and opportunists of all stripes. As for the so-called coloured people of South Africa, their identity will continue to remain fluid as long as there is the steep cultural/economic gradient between white and black which shapes all our lives.

Our task is to do away with that gradient so that all can be South Africans, even if they are also Zulu-speaking or Afrikaans-speaking, Muslim or Christian, Gautengians or *Kapenaars* (Cape residents), and so on. We have agreed, on the basis of the entire history of the world and of this country in particular, that the one identity that we will not promote is a racial identity. Hence, our intuitive rejection of any *volkstaat* (nation-state). This is precisely the problem with the identity of the so-called coloured people. Like the related "Afrikaner" identity, it is largely defined by anthropological notions of "race", rather than mainly by other markers such as language and religion.

We dream of a South Africa which is like the Great Gariep, constituted by the confluence of many different tributaries, which have their origin in different catchment areas and which are constantly changing and being changed both by the formation of new tributaries and by the backwash effects from the mainstream, which flows majestically into the great ocean of humanity. This is a more durable and a more indigenous nation than the evanescent rainbow nation, for, as we all know, there is no pot of gold at the end of the rainbow after all. Let us, then, build such a nation! ▲

Endnote

1. See Degenaar, J (1991) "The Myth of a South African Nation", Idasa Occasional Paper, No 40 (Cape Town: Idasa).

Section 6

Comparative Perspectives

Chapter 17

Diversity management in Canada

Heribert Adam
Professor of Sociology
Simon Fraser University, Vancouver, Canada

Kogila Moodley
Professor, David Lam Chair of Multi-Cultural Studies
University of British Columbia, Vancouver, Canada

The notion of autonomous individuals joined by democratic consent rather than descent still requires an emotional glue for the social contract to be obeyed. Pride in human rights adherence ... lacks the appeal and gratification that a mobilised imaginary community affords.

Multi-ethnicity and state responses

A crucial distinction must be made between two types of multi-ethnic states. The first type of state involves multi-ethnicity derived from *immigration*. This differs fundamentally from the second type, ethnic pluralism in states composed of *historical minorities* with ties to their own territory.

Immigrants do not aspire to their own state. Rather, their prime goals are economic improvement and integration without discrimination. Aspirations of diverse immigrants can best be satisfied in liberal, pluralist democracies with equal opportunities, regardless of race, origin, creed and gender. Individuals holding equal citizenship comprise the basic entities of the state and its legal system.

In contrast, a sense of national distinctiveness characterises divided societies with long-standing historical minorities. Such societies often place an imagined national good of the group above the civil rights of individuals. The group's national identity, defined by cultural boundaries, excludes those who do not share the various markers of belonging. While democratic pluralism is distinguished by the legal inclusion of all citizens, nationalist communities are closed to aliens. "Outsiders" are perceived as threatening the survival of, and laying illegitimate claims to, material entitlements. The recent stridency of nationalist movements has overwhelmed many liberal democracies and caused many a civil war, of which the former Yugoslavia is only the most reported example.

South Africa and Canada both represent divided societies with historical minorities as well as immigrants. Topping the list of Canadian concerns about equity is the integration of diverse immigrants into a traditional Anglo-French monoculture. In South Africa's case the recent influx of illegal migrants has not been articulated as an issue of integration but of deportation.

These differences, however, are overshadowed by the shared problems of separatism and regional nationalism. Quebec separatists resemble Afrikaner nationalists. And like Canada's aboriginal Indian activists, Zulu traditionalists and Western Cape voices of the "indigenous people" argue for regional autonomy, if not secession, from the central state.

After an early period of forced assimilation through missionary activity and residential schools for native children in European communities, Ottawa now favours large-scale Indian autonomy and self-government in educational and judicial matters. This abdication of responsibility for "wards of the state" on Indian reservations resembles the South African homeland policy and follows periods in Canada of benevolent tutelage and welfare colonialism that are now considered too costly.

Ironically, some Indian leaders prefer sham sovereignty, particularly where stalled negotiations about land title and treaty rights are likely to result in large payouts to relatively small bands.[1] In order to monopolise lucrative royalties from land leases, special fishing rights, gambling or oil revenues, some bands have severely restricted their membership along racist and sexist criteria. Many chiefs advocate that Indian women who marry non-Indians should forfeit their status rights.[2]

Multi-culturalism versus separate development

South African non-racialism should not mean indifference to the culture and values of the majority: a culture-neutral South African state would lose its meaning for Africans. But neither can South Africa impose majority symbols and values on sceptical minorities. Nation building in the exclusive image of the majority ("Africanisation") would alienate minorities and conjure up images of cultural totalitarianism.

In this pluralist predicament between the totalitarian temptation of enforced nation building ("one nation, one culture, one people") on the one hand and a meaningless, empty non-racialism on the other, the idea of multi-culturalism offers a synthesis.

Only Canada and Australia have adopted multi-culturalism as official state policy. Canadian multi-culturalism should not be confused with apartheid-style separate development. Apartheid aimed to exclude "outsiders" from the state while multi-culturalism strives to include new immigrants. In addition, multi-culturalism extends official recognition to all ethno-cultural or ethno-racial groups. With such symbolic outreach, Ottawa hopes to encourage identification with the state. Whereas apartheid reinforced ethnic ranking, by contrast all origins in a multi-cultural society are considered equal. Thus the policy of multi-culturalism undermined Anglo-Saxon – or in Quebec, Francophone – conformity and levelled the cultural hierarchy.

In short, five features distinguish Canadian multi-culturalism from apartheid:

- Multi-culturalism in Canada seeks to defuse conflict between the state, Quebec and First Nation groups by equalising their status with those of immigrant groups, at least symbolically. Apartheid was a plan to hierarchically order groups and incorporate them politically on a differential scale so as to facilitate greater control by the ruling group.
- Multi-culturalism in Canada redefines the hegemony of the core culture by elevating the value of cultural and linguistic diversity as worthy of celebration. Apartheid enshrined English and Afrikaans as the national core cultures and marginalised majority-group languages and symbols.
- In Canada, the term "cultures" is loosely defined as an egalitarian description referring to a wide range of immigrant groups. Under apartheid, colour and culture served the purpose of an essentialist ordering of the pigmentocracy.
- Multi-culturalism in Canada has equalising goals – if judged by the number of programmes financed to extend equality of opportunity in education, English second language instruction and equity in job opportunities. This can hardly be said of apartheid, which sought to contain differences and group ranking through entrenched unequal expenditure and opportunity.
- Inherent in multi-culturalism in Canada is the aim of promoting contact between and among groups to foster greater understanding and sharing within common institutions. By contrast, in South Africa certain kinds of interpersonal and intergroup contact were legally restricted through separate institutional structures. Apartheid, for example, impeded group interaction through educational and residential segregation while Canadian multi-culturalism seeks to foster mutual understanding in all spheres of everyday life. Culture is seldom the cause of friction. Ethno-racial culture serves merely as a marker for exclusion or entitlement.

"Rainbowism" and advocacy around the Reconstruction and Development Programme (RDP) amount to the post-apartheid version of multi-culturalism. But the "rainbow nation at peace with itself and the world", in the words of President Nelson Mandela, represents as much of an idealised fiction as the Canadian multi-ethnic family happily celebrating its diversity. Both concepts ignore the conflicts of gender, class, regionalism and ethnicity that are to be expected in every society. Rainbowism, non-racialism and multi-culturalism are intended to soothe ethno-racial tensions in an interdependent national and global economy.

Canadian multi-culturalism evades and erases issues of racism – either by denying them or adopting equity programs. Canadian equity programmes – with their four target groups of women, aboriginal people, visible minorities and the disabled – have always been voluntary, have never set quotas or timetables and have applied only to crown corporations (parastatals) and institutions with federal funding. The only mandatory aspect is annual reporting on efforts to achieve greater equity.

There is some evidence that South Africa may be spared the bitter debate about affirmative action and the ensuing backlash now taking place in North America. Sophisticated sections of the South African business sector have long recognised that it is necessary to recruit far more representatively if one is to outperform competitors and position oneself strategically in an increasingly black market. Business also accepts that it must pre-empt legislation by being seen to be more representative in a black majority culture where a black manager carries political capital with the state. Such pressure is absent where the target group is a powerless minority that depends on the goodwill of the dominant sector, as is the case in the United States and Canada.

A further point is that South African blacks do not display the same attitudes to affirmative action as do African Americans. North American public opinion holds that preferential treatment of minorities amounts to a favour. Liberal mainstream opinion maintains that minorities deserve this favour because of consistent discrimination. In South Africa, however, blacks do not see restitution as a favour but simply as a right that has long been denied.

Business against ethno-chauvinism

Nationalism characterised Europe from the 19th century until the end of World War II. But since then business has defected from the ethno-chauvinist cause in virtually every country that has a strong private sector. Previously, national-based capital backed the nationalist mobilisation for colonial expansion and imperialist competition. Now global multi-nationals are, by definition, internationalists. As George Steiner (1992) pointed out in reference to this progressive dialectic of global greed: "Great economic profit depends on crossing borders, employing people in great multi-national corporations, telling them to get along with each other."

Katharyne Mitchell (1993: 283) describes Canadian multi-culturalism as "the united colours of capitalism", accusing corporate interests of appropriating multi-cultural imagery for their own benefit. Such interest in expanding trade and the inflow of capital and skills is reflected in a renewed priority of Canadian immigration away from family reunification and refugee admission. If the Canadian economy benefits hugely from economic and cultural capital drained from abroad, colour-blindness is more "rational" than racism. These trends and social forces make ethnic and sexual chauvinism obsolete. Besides, prejudice has always correlated with class.

German critic Hans Magnus Enzensberger (1994: 121) observes that no one ever questions the freedom of movement of the rich: "For businessmen from any country, Swiss citizenship, too, is only a matter of price. No one has ever objected to the colour of the Sultan of Brunei's skin. Where bank accounts look healthy, xenophobia disappears as if by magic. But strangers are all the stranger if they are poor."

Despite the presence of such powerful interests backing non-racial colour-blindness, the management of diversity still poses severe problems. The rise of the right-wing Reform Party in Canada provides only the most obvious indicator of a continuing problem.

Ambivalence about the desirability of a multi-cultural Canada is evident given that 57 percent of citizens surveyed in a 1994 poll conducted by polling firm Angus Reid felt that Canada should "encourage minority groups to try to change to be more like most Canadians" and only 34 percent supported the idea that Canadians as a whole be encouraged "to try to accept minority groups and their customs and languages" (Reid Report, 1994: 5). Yet three-quarters of those polled seemed to take pride in the country's official policy by reaffirming that "Canada's multi-cultural make-up is one of the best things about this country" (ibid). The report states further that most Canadians are "colour blind" in the selection of immigrants and also believe that all recent immigrants should be accorded full citizenship once they have been granted entry.

On the other hand, Henry et al (1995) argue that a large majority of Canadians hold "varying degrees of racist attitudes and beliefs". However, their overt expression is mediated by vague notions of social unacceptability of such attitudes. As a result, Canada has seen the development of "democratic racism" which locates racist thought within the democratic context.

The multi-cultural fabric of Canadian society has changed dramatically in urban centres over the past decade. Between 1961 and 1991 the Canadian population rose from 18 million to 28 million. The same period coincided with a rapidly declining birth rate from 28,3 per 1 000 to 13,5 per 1 000 in 1994. In the 1970s some 180 000 immigrants were accepted annually. In the 1980s this figure increased to roughly 200 000 and in the 1990s to 250 000.

A total of 85 percent of immigrants headed for urban areas. The provinces with the highest immigration were in the west, Ontario and Quebec. Toronto attracts the largest population followed by Vancouver. In 1991, 40 percent of the populations of Vancouver and Toronto were foreign-born.

On a per capita basis, Canada takes on twice the number of immigrants as does the US and Australia. Managing diversity in these immigrant societies has increasingly resulted in similar visions. The debate focuses heavily on the question of who should define national identity and how it should be maintained in the face of increasing diversity.

Fostering public tolerance

In Canada, multi-culturalism was introduced by Pierre Trudeau's Liberals in October 1971 to placate non-English, non-French minorities whose votes were sought by all three federal parties. Multi-culturalism, in so far as it abolished the hierarchy of charter groups, also minimised the Quebecois and First Nation claims of distinct, prior rights. Quebec nationalists and native activists do not, therefore, support multi-culturalism.

Early multi-culturalism has been criticised by the Canadian Left on the grounds that it sponsors an exotic museum heritage for purposes of co-option rather than empowering immigrants. But with anti-racism and equity programmes for visible minorities increasingly at its core, multi-culturalism as state ideology has been widely accepted. It is now criticised by the political right wing as endangering national unity and wasting resources on self-styled ethnic entrepreneurs. In reality, only $25 million CAD (about R60 million) annually is spent in all three federal programmes of race relations, heritage maintenance and subsidies for ethnic activities.

Although Canadian multi-culturalism constitutes more rhetoric than substance, it fosters public tolerance. It bestows an aura of respectability to difference. It legitimises minority spokespersons as recognised partners of government – to their mutual benefit. Ethnic entrepreneurs and employers of the tolerance industry gain status and small subsidies while state officials wallow in the good feeling that they have reached out to others.

De-nationalisation instead of nation building?

Canadian and South African nationalism face the impossible task of representing the people as one. Given these countries' divided history, lack of unifying symbols and the strength of sub-national heritage, European-type nation building amounts to a divisive exercise. Quebec separatists or Native Indian activists – like Zulu traditionalists or Afrikaner nationalists – cultivate distrust of the unifying attempts of the centre.

If South Africa were to follow the European model of homogenisation, that would mean centralisation that is unacceptable to at least a quarter of its population. On the other hand, if South Africa were to follow the Canadian model of multi-culturalism, it risks perpetuating apartheid-imposed ethno-racial divisions. The ethno-racial groups in South Africa were state-created and state-sponsored, unlike Canada where ethno-racial groups are self-chosen and therefore not discredited. Should ethno-racial groups also mobilise voluntarily in the post-apartheid era, this would still take place under the apartheid-created labels and boundaries. South Africa can neither adopt the European way of "moulding Italians after creating Italy" nor embrace the Canadian or Australian way of fostering ethno-racial heritages.

South Africa has to pursue a third route of state-building. This could nevertheless borrow selected techniques for the management of diversity from elsewhere. One option for a third route could aim at de-nationalising the state. Just as church and state were strictly separated in the New World in order to avoid the export of religious strife from the Old World, so a consciously de-nationalised state would resemble its secular variety on issues of nation building. It would be a "non-nation nation". At the most, a denationalised state could mediate between ethno-racial groups within its borders and keep the peace.

However, a de-ethnicised state as neutral arbitrator may be as unrealistic in South Africa as the postulated colour blindness of citizens in a liberal democracy. The notion of autonomous individuals joined by democratic consent rather than descent still requires an emotional glue for the social contract to be obeyed. Pride in human rights adherence, development or the equality provided by a model democracy in place of nationalism, as recommended by Johan Degenaar (1991), lacks the appeal and gratification that a mobilised imagined community affords, even only fleetingly, during a rugby game.

Furthermore, rights of citizenship rest on limited resources. The RDP, like the Western welfare state, cannot allow free access. Open borders and the abolition of citizenship is utopian at present. But South Africa, like Germany, would benefit from a rational immigration policy while granting the universal rights of democracy to all its permanent inhabitants.

The most important lesson for ethnic conflict management from experiences abroad is the promotion of centre-region contracts. This involves allowing non-sessionist forms of self-determination and self-rule with the possibility of unilateral decision making, exclusive powers and substantial autonomy for distinct regions and/or sub-groups.

A high degree of genuine federalism and organisational decentralisation does not threaten the unity of a state and political parties but guarantees cohesion by pre-empting splits and ethno-national mobilisation. Had Canada recognised Quebec as a distinct founding nation with special rights, Quebec separatists would have had the wind taken out of their sails long ago.

Nationalism thrives on rejection and suppression. Central control is often counter-productive. In the South African context that means the following: had the Western Cape African National Congress (ANC) been allowed to choose its leadership according to local conditions and preferences instead of having to follow headquarters' choices in personnel and policy priorities, it could have avoided an embarrassing organisational split and popular rejection of its top candidate.[3]

In a similar vein, is it wise to continue to demonise the Inkatha Freedom Party's (IFP) leadership and denounce its substantial support in KwaZulu-Natal as fraudulent? Attempts to buy off IFP-supporting chiefs or restrict their power by granting permanent land tenure in rural areas seem as short-sighted and unsuccessful as similar co-option attempts by apartheid social engineers.

The central dispute between the ANC and IFP concerns the degree of pluralism allowed, or what IFP leader Chief Mangosuthu Buthelezi perceives as ANC attempts to "flatten diversity and to bring it under its control or to destroy it" (*Sunday Tribune*, 30 July 1995).

A supreme irony asserts itself in post-apartheid South Africa: the funeral of formal apartheid has been accompanied by the increasing legitimacy of ethno-racialism. An anti-apartheid government that extolls a colour-blind non-racialism as its core ideology is nonetheless confronted with renewed ethnic consciousness. The struggle against ethnicising apartheid was to herald a "raceless" society. Its alleged triumph has to come to terms not only with the historical legacy of racial indoctrination but also with renewed ethno-racial claims for differential entitlement. ▲

Endnotes

1. "Bands" is the term used by native communities to distinguish themselves from neighbouring groups. Bands form "tribal councils" which have their own language or cultural tradition. There are over 600 Indian groups in Canada clamouring for some form of sovereignty and aboriginal rights as "First Nations".

2. For example, the membership code adopted in 1981 by the Kahnasetake Mohawk band calls for a moratorium on mixed marriages and a "blood quantum" to measure the racial purity of a resident. The federal Indian Act has also used a 50 percent quotient in deciding who is a status Indian. The Mohawk committee has sent out some 100 expulsion notices to residents since 1990 in order to "purify the Mohawk blood line". In July 1995, Federal Court Justice Frank Muldoon compared this "eugenic tyranny" with Nazi practices (*Globe & Mail*, 10 July 1995).

3. Wilmot James's (*Democracy in Action*, Vol 9, No 3, June 1995) apt question has yet to be answered: "Is political authority derived from presidential annointment or does it require some resonance with democratic criteria and electoral credibility?"

References

Bissoondath, N (1994) *Selling Illusions: The Cult of Multi-Culturalism in Canada* (Toronto: Penguin).

Dryden, PL (1993) "Multi-culturalism and the development of Canadian immigration and refugee policy", unpublished paper.

Degenaar, J (1991) "The Myth of a South African Nation", Idasa Occasional Paper, No 40 (Cape Town: Idasa).

Enzensberger, HM (1994) *Civil Wars* (London: Granta Books).

Fieras, A and JL Elliott (1992) *Multi-Culturalism in Canada* (Scarborough: Nelson Canada).

Gillroy, P (1992) "The end of anti-racism", in J Donald and A Rattansi (eds) *Race, Culture and Difference* (London: Sage).

Henry, F, C Tator, W Mattish and T Rees (1995) *The Colour of Democracy: Racism in Canadian Society* (Toronto: Harcourt Press).

Ley, D (1995) "Between Europe and Asia: The case of the missing sequoias", in *Ecumene*, Vol 2, No 2.

Mitchell, K (1993) "Multi-culturalism or the United Colors of Capitalism?" in *Antipode*, Vol 25, No 4.

Moodley, K (1983) "Canadian multi-culturalism as ideology", in *Ethnic and Racial Studies*, Vol 6, No 3.

Moodley, K (1984) "The predicament of racial affirmative action: A critical review of equality now", in *Queen's Quarterly*, Vol 91, No 4.

Reid, A (1994) "Tolerance and the Canadian Ethno-cultural Mosaic", in *The Reid Report*, Vol 9, No 4.

Steiner, G (1992) "Voices from the New Europe", in *CBC Ideas*, 1 June 1992.

Chapter 18

Outlawing discrimination in Britain

Kamlesh Bahl
Chairperson
Equal Opportunities Commission of Great Britain

When voluntary action and government exhortations proved to be inadequate responses to tackling deep-seated prejudices, British policy makers decided that a legal framework was needed.

Background

Various political instruments have been used in Britain to manage and regulate diversity. British legislation provides for positive measures to counteract the effects of past discrimination and to help remove the impression that certain training opportunities or jobs are reserved solely for one gender or for the majority racial group.

This has not, however, always been the case. In 1970 the first piece of legislation was passed to outlaw unequal pay for men and women doing the same job. Prior to this the common law had no mechanism to counter gender and racial inequality. Thus, although the Britain of the 1960s was viewed by many as a time of freedom, the freedom to discriminate was also in evidence.

It was commonplace to see in industry and commerce a special wage rate for women which was below the lowest wage paid to men. Black women fared especially badly in this regard. Women, blacks and other ethnic minorities were virtually absent from the judiciary, senior levels of organisations in the public and private sector, police and parliament.

There had been some voluntary action to tackle inequality. Equal pay for men and women performing the same job was implemented by the civil service during the previous decade. Furthermore, during the era of full employment that characterised Britain in the 1960s, most blacks who wanted to work were able to find jobs. But these tended to be in either lowly paid industries such as transport, hotels and catering or in occupations which had lower rates of pay because they were filled mainly by women, blacks and ethnic minorities rather than white men.

When voluntary action and government exhortations proved to be inadequate responses to tackling deep-seated prejudices, British policy makers decided that a legal framework was needed.

Legal framework: racial discrimination

Britain has no laws which expressly penalise people according to their race or colour. As long as individuals satisfy rules about nationality and residence, members of all races may vote, travel on public transport and apply for the benefits of education, employment and social services. However, the Race Relations Act of 1976 is considered necessary for the protection of those who are liable to be treated less favourably because of their colour, race, ethnic or national origins.

The Act protects people defined by reference to cultural traditions and community perceptions rather than by strict reference to biology. Thus if a group of people regard themselves as a distinct racial group as a result of common history, social actions, language or religion, its members can invoke this Act to combat discrimination based on membership of the group.

The Act entitles them to bring proceedings if they have been subjected to less favourable treatment than members of other racial groups in a wide range of situations where discrimination has proved a serious problem. The first area is in the provision of goods, facilities or services. This covers places of public entertainment or refreshment such as dance halls, theatres, cinemas, cafes and public libraries. The Act covers access to hotels, boarding houses and transport as well as businesses and professions which provide services to the public (doctors and estate agents selling property, for example). It also prohibits employers from discriminating along race lines during recruitment by refusing an applicant employment or by giving him or her different terms of employment or opportunities for training or promotion. It is also unlawful for trade unions to discriminate by denying membership or refusing benefits to people from particular racial groups. The legislation has been widely used to successfully challenge discrimination in these areas.

The most important innovation in the 1976 Act was to outlaw the indirect discrimination which occurs where a condition applies in theory to all racial groups but when in practice a far smaller proportion from one racial group can comply with it than the proportion from other groups. The concept was imported from American law where it was founded on a United States Supreme Court ruling on a condition requiring applicants for manual work at a power station to have graduated from high school or to have passed an IQ test to measure intelligence. The court found that the condition discriminated in practice against blacks and could not be justified as a necessary qualification for the job.

Vitally important for the protection of individual rights and the elimination of discrimination was the establishment through the Race Relations Act of the Commission for Racial Equality, an independent statutory body with powers to enforce the law in the public interest and to promote good race relations. The Act also places a duty on local government institutions to eliminate discrimination and to promote good race relations.

The law cannot produce racial harmony but it can remove causes of tension and grievance, and provide redress. The Act has served an educative purpose and has broken down barriers for individuals fortunate or courageous enough to use it. But the powers of the Commission for Racial Equality to investigate discrimination against groups of people have been limited by court decisions. For example, the commission cannot investigate an organisation unless it already has evidence to suspect that unlawful discrimination is taking place.

Legal framework: gender discrimination

The Sex Discrimination Act of 1975 contains most of the provisions of the Race Relations Act described above. The original Act contained several exclusions relating to, for example, pensions, small businesses employing fewer than six people and employment in the armed forces. Many of these have been successfully challenged and removed by the use of European Community (EC) law, which has seen a number of binding directives issued to member states.

The existence of the independent Equal Opportunities Commission (EOC) has also enabled strategic legal action to be taken to broaden the scope of the legislation and the amount of protection enjoyed by individuals. For example, sexual harassment of a woman at work is unlawful under the Act as the courts ruled in an EOC test case that it amounted to less favourable treatment on the grounds of gender.

Another example is that the EOC took judicial review proceedings against the Minister for Employment on the grounds that Britain's employment protection laws indirectly discriminated against women by not providing the same levels of protection for part-time workers as for full-time workers. The commission argued that this was indirect discrimination since women constituted 86 percent of part-time workers. The courts agreed and the law was changed to extend protection to more than 600 000 employees.

A third example of how the EOC, as an independent guardian of the law, and the provisions of EC law have intersected is the EOC-supported test case by Helen Marshall to the European Court of Justice. This case determined that the level of compensation then available in British tribunals – a maximum of 11 000 (about R62 150) – was inadequate to compensate Marshall for the discrimination she had suffered. The government of the United Kingdom subsequently removed the upper limit. Since that decision nearly two years ago, awards have increased sevenfold and employers have become far more willing to settle claims without going to court. Thus the law is now a genuine deterrent to discriminatory acts.

Lessons

It is vital to enact laws which provide effective rights to individuals and effective sanctions against discrimination. These laws need to be accessible rather than rights which exist only on paper. In addition, the existence of an independent, properly resourced agency to help enforce the law and promote equality is invaluable.

In Britain the legal frameworks dealing with race and gender discrimination are the most developed areas. A bill to outlaw discrimination against disabled people is currently going through parliament but this will only outlaw discrimination in the employment field.

While the bill is a welcome development, the failure to set up a disability commission has been criticised by many observers, including the EOC. It is also commonplace for the equal opportunities policies of organisations to prohibit discrimination on the grounds of sexual orientation and age, although there are no statutory rights in these areas.

Positive action

Positive action refers to a variety of measures designed to tackle the effects of past discrimination and, in practical terms, to enable individuals to compete on the same basis for employment. It may include special training programmes to enable members of the under-represented gender or racial group to acquire skills which will allow them to compete in the job market with the over-represented group. It makes lawful the special encouragement of an under-represented group to apply for jobs in which members of the group have been under-represented in the previous 12 months.

The main aim of positive action is to make equal opportunity a reality. Even if gender and racial discrimination could be removed overnight, women and ethnic minority employees and job applicants would still suffer the effects of past discrimination and disadvantage. For example:

- Ethnic minority men and women in Britain are more likely to be unemployed and in lower graded jobs than their white counterparts. Research for the EOC shows that black women receive four-fifths of white women's pay. This is due to the effects of past and continuing discrimination. In addition, there is on average a 20 percent pay gap between women and men in full-time work.
- Even if selection criteria and appointment procedures are corrected to remove direct and indirect discrimination, it will still take many years to redress the effects of past discrimination. Positive action is therefore intended to accelerate the process whereby women and ethnic minority employees are able to apply and compete for jobs on the same basis as men and the ethnic majority.

Positive action is often confused with positive discrimination and affirmative action. In Britain, decision making at the point of selection must be free from discrimination. This means that positive discrimination is unlawful. The EOC supports this approach in the context of the culture and traditions in British society. It is clear that positive discrimination on the grounds of sex or race would not be supported by the wider population and could spark a backlash.

An interesting recent experience in this regard involves the major opposition party in Britain, the Labour Party. It is important to note here that the activities of political parties are excluded from the provisions of the Sex Discrimination Act. The Labour Party adopted a policy of identifying a percentage of seats for which women-only short lists should be drawn up for the selection of candidates to fight the next general election. This was a measure designed to improve the representation of women in parliament (currently just under 10 percent). At least one legal challenge to the policy is now being made. The policy received little publicity when it was drawn up two years ago, but more recently, where men have been discriminated against during implementation of the policy, much public debate has ensued. Indications are that the policy will be discontinued after the next general election.

Components of a positive action programme

What we are seeing in recent years is far greater use of targets, or goals, for equality which are based on achieving progress over time. Targets are a major way in which diversity is being managed in large and medium enterprises in Britain.

One of the highest profile examples is the campaign by a number of leading public and private employers called "Opportunity 2000" which aims to significantly increase the number of women in senior positions by the end of the decade.

As the result of two decades spent working towards the elimination of discrimination, the EOC has formulated five steps which it deems crucial to the success of a positive action programme:

- Positive action, whether as training or as encouragement, is best undertaken within the framework of an equal opportunities policy and programme to manage diversity.
- Schemes must have the commitment of senior managers who must decide what action to take, middle managers who carry the responsibility of communicating to employees, and employees who need to understand that a positive action initiative enhances individual potential without disadvantaging anyone.
- All those involved need to know what measures are planned and why. Care must be taken to consult the minority group in question before introducing any measure. Members of minority groups may be understandably wary of action which suggests preferential treatment or tokenism. The EOC experience is that people want the opportunity to compete on merit rather than be given special treatment.
- Good communication and effective planning are essential throughout the process to avoid misunderstandings and complaints.
- Monitoring of the whole programme is essential. At the beginning, it allows sensible targets to be set; during the programme it allows progress to be reviewed and changes made if necessary; at the end, it evaluates the success of the initiative and determines whether further action is needed.

Examples of positive action

A range of positive action initiatives have been implemented in Britain to tackle racial and sexual inequalities. These include:

- Many employers have stopped recruiting staff through word-of-mouth recommendation from the existing work-force. The reason is that if the work-force is over-representative of one racial group or gender then other members of that group are likely to be contacted when vacancies arise. Increasingly, employers use positive action advertising which includes advertising in media which target ethnic minority groups.

- A number of colleges and community projects have developed "preparation for work" training schemes to meet the special needs of particular racial groups. Such schemes have provided training in industrial, language and communications skills.
- Job grading schemes to determine pay have been reviewed in a number of organisations to ensure that the knowledge and skills possessed by individuals whose work involves dealing with different racial groups is not under-valued. Such skills would be rated on a par with technical knowledge or in-depth knowledge of other parts of the business.
- Government departments and providers of services increasingly produce publications in a range of ethnic minority languages. Trade unions have co-operated with colleges to develop courses to equip members of under-represented racial groups with the practical skills needed to participate fully in the running of trade unions which in Britain have traditionally been white, male institutions.

Key concepts

In Britain the latest thinking on equality includes two important concepts. The first is to try to make issues of equality part of mainstream thinking and to factor these into the daily decision-making processes of national and local government, employers and other providers.

"Mainstreaming", as it is known, requires training of managers and decision makers to raise their awareness of equality issues. A conscious effort is needed to ensure that such issues are considered and individual programmes monitored. One could examine, for example, whether those benefiting from publicly funded training schemes constituted a representative profile of the wider population.

The second concept is that of checking proposals for new legislation for any potentially adverse impact on one gender or racial group. At present, the British parliament receives an assessment of the public expenditure implications of new legislation. The EOC would like to see that approach extended to include the implications for gender and race discrimination. It has also called for all official statistics to be broken down by gender and, where possible, by ethnic origin, age and disability. This would be a fundamental step in effective monitoring of government policy. For example, certain earnings statistics concerning lowly paid workers are not broken down to show the hourly rate of pay for women and men.

The development and evaluation of public policy on inequality needs to be informed by adequate statistical information. The debate should be a public one and with this in mind the EOC has called for a regular annual debate in parliament on the progress being made towards equality.

Such proposals are contained in a National Agenda for Action which covers political, social, economic and health issues and has been drawn up by the EOC in partnership with the Commission for Northern Ireland and the Women's National Commission. The agenda will be used to ensure that action is taken by government and to provide a checklist to measure the commitment of political parties to equality issues as Britain approaches its next general election and to measure progress on equality over the coming years.

Conclusion

Equality entails enabling each individual to achieve his or her full potential as well as enabling the best use of resources to compete effectively in an increasingly global marketplace. Over the past two decades, Britain has seen the introduction of major political initiatives on managing diversity. Equality of opportunity is increasingly supported by employers and trade unions despite the difficult economic period experienced in Britain during the early 1990s.

As gender and race discrimination have become established as threats to fundamental human rights, and as the business and economic case for the elimination of discrimination is increasingly recognised, calls are now being made to outlaw other forms of discrimination. ▲

Chapter 19

Diversity and assimilation in Brazil

Fernando Rosa Ribeiro
Centre for Afro-Asian Studies,
Rio de Janeiro, Brazil

Unity was achieved at the price of stigmatising and dis-criminating against a large percentage of the population. But as the assimilationist ideology has spread throughout the society, it cannot easily be displaced.

A colour-coded society

Comparing Brazil with countries outside Latin America is a tricky undertaking, especially if the comparison involves countries such as South Africa, Britain, Canada or the United States.

One reason is that "race" and "ethnicity" were historically constructed in Brazil in a different way. In the case of race, for instance, in Brazil "white", "black" and "coloured" have not been used as essentialist categories as occurred in South Africa where these terms were constructed to define supposedly separate, self-contained categories, each having its own identity in terms of biology, culture, language and so on.

In fact, race has not been a term of popular discourse in Brazil. Instead people talk about colour, not race – and the difference is great: colour stands for appearance (say skin colour, nose shape and hair type) as opposed to an inner essence that is supposedly contained in one's blood. Consequently, neither the government nor society at large has constructed the so-called races as well-bound entities which are clearly distinguishable one from the other.

Towards assimilation

Instead of racial separation, Brazil's history has been one of assimilation of different others within a common national space. This assimilationist framework has rested on the premise of blood-mixing. In the 19th century, Brazil was mostly a mixed-race nation. Faced with European racial theories of the time proclaiming that a mixed-race nation would never amount to much, the Brazilian elite decided to sponsor mass European immigration with the purpose of whitening the nation. The practice started in the latter quarter of the 19th century.

The result of this mass immigration (second only to European immigration to the United States) tipped the demographic balance towards the white element for the early decades of this century. The idea, however, was not to whiten the nation by swamping it with immigrants who would oust the local population but rather to let the former mix their blood with the latter. It was hoped that this would eventually create a population that appeared white and homogeneous. When overall blood-mixing (called miscegenation in Brazil) had taken place, Brazil would be a "proper" nation because it would be both racially and ethnically homogeneous as well as fair-skinned. In other words, Brazil would become homogeneous because it would be a nation of thoroughly mixed blood.

The assimilationist project has been fairly deep-rooted. Contrary to what happens in the US, for instance, black Brazilians for the most part do not take on a black identity. And contrary to what happens in South Africa, ethnic claims to distinctness and separateness have been historically stifled. Except for the country's tiny Native South American Indian minority (less than one percent of the total population), no groups have had homelands or separate territories, nor have they claimed any.

Although some areas are whiter or blacker than others (the south is more European whereas the north-east is blacker), there has been no urban or rural segregation in Brazil as occurred in South Africa during apartheid. Overall, people of different colour have more or less lived in contact and inter-married to a fairly large extent throughout Brazilian history.

Nowadays, using the census colour categories, it can be ascertained that around 20 percent of all marriages in Brazil are mixed marriages. (The equivalent figure for the US is two to three percent.)[1]

Inequality and discrimination

Does this mean that Brazil is a racial paradise when compared to South Africa or the US? Many have claimed so in the past, particularly the famous Brazilian sociologist Gilberto Freyre whose works have been widely translated and read throughout the world. In the not so distant past, Brazil successfully managed to transmit to the world the image of a country free of racial and ethnic strife.

Though there is some substance to this image, it is not entirely truthful. Firstly, the genocide of Indian populations continues in the Amazon. Secondly, an examination of census figures reveals glaring inequalities in income between blacks, whites and what the census calls brown or *pardo*.

For instance, although uneducated blacks, browns and whites are positioned at the bottom of the wage pyramid, whites with at least 11 years of schooling tend to earn 80 percent more than blacks or browns.[2] So in spite of the absence of formal wage discrimination between races in Brazil, somehow the better paid jobs end up in white hands. Also, in the highest income groups, the appearance of the population is clearly on the whiter side with few black faces.

In terms of everyday interaction, a person who is very dark-skinned is far more likely to be harassed by the police or badly treated at a government office. This is in spite of the outlawing of discrimination by the Brazilian Constitution of 1988 and an absence of the type of formal discrimination that existed in South Africa and the US.

Discrimination and colour prejudice are widespread in Brazil. Nonetheless, due to the different nature of the historically constructed vision of diversity in that country, it cannot be addressed in terms familiar to North Americans and South Africans. An example of this is that affirmative action or equity along North American lines has not been feasible. This is because of the grip which the ideology of assimilation and whitening holds over the social imagination of Brazilians. Rather than an ideology sponsored by the state and a minority elite, as apartheid was, assimilationism has spread throughout the society and all races subscribe to it.

There are several reasons for this. One is the historical lack of a segregationist system in Brazil based on the assumption that races or ethnic groups are wholly separate entities with an identity, language and culture of their own. The assimilationist framework ensured that the elite's values spread to the whole society. National unity in Brazil was achieved at the price of spreading the elite's somatic norm – that is, looking white is considered to be the norm – to the whole society.

The consequences of this were several. Firstly, the black somatic norm became the most undesirable one and was therefore stigmatised. This ensured that blacks in Brazil did not take it on as a self-designation. In the 1990 census survey, only 4,9 percent of the population declared themselves to be black (Programa Nacional de Amostra Domiciliar, 1990, Instituto Brasileiro de Geografia e Estatística, Rio).

People who are very dark-skinned in Brazil usually resent being called black and prefer a range of other (more or less euphemistic) terms of self-classification – dark, brown, *bonbom* brown, chocolate and so on.[3] Almost anything goes as long as you do not classify yourself with a stigmatised term such as black.

The census categories (black, brown, white and yellow) do not actually reflect self-classification. Also, unlike South Africa, racial classification was never compulsory in Brazil in this century. Nonetheless, it is interesting to examine the census results. In the 1990 census survey only 4,9 percent of people declared themselves to be black, 55,3 percent declared themselves to be white, 39,3 percent brown and 0,5 percent yellow (or Asian).

Anyone who has been to Brazil has reason to doubt such results. These seem instead to be a direct reflection of the ideology of whitening, namely, that people tend to classify themselves with a lighter hue than they possess. The figure for whites seems particularly inflated, although as compulsory race classification has not existed, it is hard to say how inflated.

Another consequence of this system is that Brazil's black movements are tiny and politically unimportant. They have historically failed to become mass movements because they have been unable to convince their potential constituency of their blackness.

Shifting sands of politics

The lack of clear boundaries between the "races" parallels a similar lack of boundaries in other domains. For instance, Brazilian politics has not usually been as neatly polarised as in South African or North American politics. In the past, Brazil has been ruled mostly by an elite. Historically, this elite has not been seen as a settler elite, nor as an exclusively white elite, but simply as the rich or powerful.

Traditionally, political parties in Brazil could not be distinguished by their different ideological positions (conservative, liberal or leftist, for example) but by the fact that they represented different factions of the elite. This still applies to a large extent, although the appearance of the Workers' Party in 1978 (a mass-based party with a clear ideological line) has changed the political climate somewhat.

It would be unthinkable for a situation to occur in South Africa whereby millions of voters shifted their allegiance from the African National Congress to the National Party in the next election. But in the last national and regional elections in Brazil that is exactly what happened. Within a few months (from May to October 1994) tens of millions of voters shifted their preferences from the Workers' Party-led coalition to Fernando Henrique Cardosa (who was inaugurated in January 1995 as president of Brazil). That the shift occurred mainly due to the perceived success of Cardosa's economic policies as minister of finance in the previous government is not entirely irrelevant in a country torn for years by deep economic crisis and hyperinflation.

Yet the shift showed that there are few captive constituencies in Brazil. Voters have to be won anew at each election. Also, Brazilian voters cast a highly personalised vote: they tend to vote for individuals rather than for parties. A common occurrence is that a voter will vote in a single election for different candidates from widely different parties competing for different positions (say, a senator will come from one party, a member of the chamber of deputies from another, a governor from a third party and so on).

The cost of national unity

A common society is not an aspiration in Brazil as it is in South Africa, where the population is striving to promote national unity. The assimilationist project, with its roots in the 19th century, is consequently neither a new nor a politically self-conscious, self-serving project as was apartheid. No political party – not even the Workers' Party – seriously contests it. Rather than a clear policy pursued with a vengeance by a minority, it has become the basis for national unity in Brazil.

The unfortunate side to this is that unity was achieved at the price of stigmatising and discriminating against a large percentage of the population. But because the assimilationist ideology has spread throughout the society, it cannot be easily displaced. This makes the fight against discrimination more difficult than is the case in countries such as South Africa.

Also, the struggle against inequality in Brazil – on the basis of race, gender, sexual orientation or class – is pursued within an overall framework that perhaps does not allow enough space for separate identities to emerge. Brazil does not have to confront separatist claims of any kind or any deep-seated division within the body of the nation. But the country does have to confront an entrenched practice of inequality within a framework that at present may not provide enough room for the acknowledgement of either diversity or inequality.

When compared to South Africa, Brazil has a clear edge in the domain of national unity. Yet in the arena of social change, Brazil may be at a disadvantage. ▲

Endnotes

1. Dr Carlos Hasenbalg, Centre for Afro-Asian Studies, Rio, personal communication.

2. "Os números da cor: boletim estatístico sobre a situaçao sócio-econômica dos grupos de cor no Brasil e em suas regioes", Centre for Afro-Asian Studies, Rio de Janeiro, 1995.

3. A 1976 census survey uncovered 134 terms used in self-designation spanning the gamut from black to white (PNAD 1976, IBGE, Rio de Janeiro).

Chapter 20

Power sharing
in Malaysia

Mavis Putchucheary
Consultant and former lecturer in political science
University of Malaysia

*The Malaysian experience has shown that it is precisely be-
cause of the existence of a democratic system, albeit in a
truncated form, that the country has enjoyed the high rate
of economic growth since independence.*

Introduction

Malaysia is an example of a multi-ethnic society which devised a strategy soon after its independence for inter-ethnic co-operation through a consociational arrangement in which the major
groups in society are represented in a "grand coalition".

Such an arrangement recognises the potent force of cultural pluralism and provides structures for political elites to co-operate while allowing the different communities to be represented
through their own ethnic-based organisations. Minorities who fear that their interests will not be
adequately protected in a non-ethnic party structure may feel more secure if they are represented
by their own ethnic leaders.

In Malaysia, the pattern of cultural diversity can best be described as bipolar in that two main
groups – Malays and non-Malays (mainly Chinese and Indians) – of more or less equal size are
pitted against each other. This pattern has made a consociational arrangement necessary, where
parties share executive power on the basis of proportional representation and minority parties
have a veto right on certain critical issues.

However, this consociational arrangement is also extraordinarily diffi﹍ ﹍. as there is a danger of each side seeing no reason to accommodate the other since each hopes to gain control of government. Electoral competition is likely to be so intense that it produces ethnic outbidding. In this situation, ethnic-based structures may be the only way of achieving some form of accommodation to prevent the total polarisation of conflict.

The consociational arrangement does not assume that there is equal political strength between ethnic groups represented in the coalition. Rather, it recognises that differentials in group strength may exist and tries to prevent any one group from becoming dominant or capturing the state through a power-sharing system. However, the considerable variation in the strength of ethnic identities soon developed into Malay political hegemony – a situation which the consociational model was designed to avoid. The leaders of the dominant group, the Malays, began to claim political superiority on the basis of their claim to be the indigenous people or the *Bumiputeras* ("sons of the soil"). This claim was rooted in the argument that the country historically belonged to the Malays and that the arrival and settlement of the Chinese and Indians during the colonial period did not mean that these "immigrants" had the same rights as Malays.

Nevertheless, the coalition arrangement did provide incentives for ethnic accommodation in the sense that both sides appeared willing to put aside, for the time being, their earlier demands: Malays for exclusive political rights as the "indigenous" people, and non-Malays for equal political rights with Malays.

Timing proved to be as important as the strategy for inter-ethnic co-operation. Co-operation between the United Malay National Organisation (UMNO) and the Malayan Chinese Association (MCA) began first at the local government level. By the time the first national elections were held in 1955, the alliance coalition – made up of the UMNO and MCA initially and then the Malaysian Indian Congress – had already been formed.

The leaders of these parties were tied together in bonds of mutual dependence. UMNO leaders depended on the MCA to convince the British that power was being transferred to all segments of society and MCA leaders were aware that they could not form the government on their own. As a "middleman minority" vulnerable to charges of exploitation by the indigenous leadership, Chinese leaders generally preferred to be in the government where they could influence political decision making than in the opposition.

Impact on democracy

Hegemony and democracy are incompatible. While democracy lays down the formal rules of the game but does not guarantee winning for any group, hegemony often manipulates the democratic rules to ensure winning. This was seen in 1989 when Malaysia's ruling elite, faced with a serious threat to its hegemony because it failed to secure legitimacy from within its own ethnic group, dismantled the democratic system in favour of an authoritarian regime. Although democracy was restored after almost two years, it was clear that the formal rules for fair electoral conduct could be perverted and manipulated to entrench the ruling class in power.

The principle of "rural weightage" was used to ensure that there were many more Malay-majority constituencies than non-Malay majority constituencies, thus further bolstering Malay hegemony. In a single-member, first-past-the-post electoral system it is essential for the constituencies to be of equal size. In Malaysia this is not the case. For example, it is estimated that the largest (urban) constituency is about five times larger than the smallest (rural) constituency. In this way, the non-Malay vote is reduced in electoral strength in favour of the Malay vote.

Political stability

Under certain circumstances, political hegemony can ensure political stability. By involving the leadership of each group in a relationship, even though one is dominant, the system can provide benefits to all sections of society. In Malaysia, patronage is distributed through party and government channels. For example, shares in newly restructured companies which are to be floated in the open market at greatly deflated prices are allocated to all political parties in the ruling coalition. *Bumiputera* companies are given preference in the allocation of these shares as Malays are under-represented in business, but non-*Bumiputera* companies are not excluded.

At an individual level, the rule of law applies to government as well as to private individuals and companies. It appears that once its political hegemony had been firmly entrenched, the ruling elite was more willing to establish a political system in which all people could enjoy equal protection under the law. The ideals of democracy – at least in terms of the rule of law, freedom of worship and protection of private property – were maintained once the government had secured a reasonably broad-based legitimacy.

This legitimacy was secured by holding relatively free and fair elections at regular intervals. The leadership now has considerable autonomy to govern in the interests of the country as a whole and not just pander to the interests of its party supporters. Although coercive means cannot be ruled out, the main form of social control is through persuasion and collaboration.

Ethnic relations and economic development

Following the economic successes of the East Asian countries, there has been a growing literature advocating that a strong government is an essential prerequisite for economic development. While not rejecting democracy, these advocates suggest that democracy without economic development cannot be sustained. The government has a responsibility to direct the course of economic development as its top priority, and democracy will have to be put on the back-burner for the time being.

But the Malaysian experience has shown that it is precisely because of the existence of a democratic system, albeit in a truncated form, that the country has enjoyed the high rate of economic growth since independence. Business was dominated by non-Malays, mainly by the Chinese. Thus the government, in order to gain relatively broad political support, was compelled to work closely with non-Malay business groups to develop economic policies that brought about this growth.

The system is effective in that potential or actual ethnic conflict is managed by ensuring that all significant groups benefit from economic development. The New Economic Policy (NEP) adopted by the government contained an ambitious programme of affirmative action to promote businesses owned by Malays. The government was expected to play a direct role in the economy to implement this affirmative action programme, but when faced with an economic and financial crisis in the mid-1980s, it had the capacity and support to make politically unpopular decisions to stimulate economic growth.

In the long run, economic growth produced a non-zero-sum game situation where both Malays and non-Malays could benefit. Although the NEP has given rise to considerable inter-ethnic and intra-ethnic tension, on the whole the programme has been implemented in a gradual manner in order not to put too large a strain on the delicate balance of power between the non-Malay business community and the politically dominant Malays.

State impact on ethnic relations

While it cannot be denied that economic growth is an essential ingredient for ethnic harmony, it is only in the negative sense that equating economic development with ethnic harmony is valid. Declining rates of economic growth often result in unemployment, increasing poverty and high inflation rates which tend to exacerbate ethnic conflict.

But this does not mean that economic development automatically results in a reduction of ethnic conflict. As the Malaysian example shows, a sense of relative deprivation may be felt among individuals and groups even during periods of economic prosperity.

To the extent that social cohesion depends on economic growth, there are bound to be problems. The omnipotent state may find that, despite its increasing powers, its capacity to bring about a "fair" distribution of resources between ethnic groups may have declined. This is because the impact of economic growth on the relative strength of ethnic and class-based groups in society may have unintended consequences. For example, economic growth may have increased the resources available to the Chinese, resulting in greater dissatisfaction among certain sections within the Malay community who believe they are not acquiring their "fair" share of economic growth. At the same time among non-Malays there is also a sense of grievance resulting from the deepening conviction of "unfairness" about the way state resources are distributed.

This has resulted in a hardening of ethnic positions by both groups. Although high levels of economic growth have muted ethnic antagonisms to some extent, this does not mean that Malaysia has solved its ethnic problems.

As several writers have observed, the absence of ethnic strife does not mean that there is ethnic harmony. Unless political institutions aimed at ensuring fair rules of the democratic game are developed and the state is tamed by the constitutionalisation of state-civil society relationships, a high potential for ethnic conflict will continue to plague Malaysian society. The increasing authoritarianism of the state in more recent years also reflects the reduced capacity of the state to manage conflict.

An important lesson to be learned from the Malaysian experience is that the state may, by its own actions, intensify rather than reduce conflict. Despite the "mixed" strategy approach adopted by the state, it has failed to construct a public ideology in which all cultural groups can find a place. In its quest for a post-apartheid political order, South Africa can do well by learning from the successes as well as the mistakes of Malaysia. ▲

References

Horowitz, D (1989) "Cause and Consequence in the Public Policy Theory", in *Public Policies*, Vol 22.

Loh, KW and JS Kahn (1992) "Introduction", in *Fragmented Vision* (Sydney: Allen and Unwin).

Young, C (June 1991) "Comparative Reflections on Ethnic Conflict", unpublished paper presented at a United Nations Research Institute for Social Development conference on Ethnic Conflict, Dubrovnik.

Conclusion

Executive director
Institute for Democracy in South Africa

Daria Caliguire
Researcher
Institute for Democracy in South Africa

The primary mission of Idasa is to assist in the consolidation of our recently formed democracy. In more specific terms, it is to assist in empowering individuals and institutions in a manner that makes the framework created in 1994 a viable and sustainable one. We think the tensions and emergent conflicts in the Western Cape, the nuances of which are discussed in some length in this book, are a threat to the consolidation of democratic institutions.

The context of the book is the democratic transition, which is based on reconciliation and maximum inclusiveness – hence the government of national unity (GNU) and minority representation in the institutions of governance.

We should remind ourselves of the benefits of the democratic transition and the benefits that the GNU has brought. Our new democracy is both the culmination of decades of conflict and struggle – to which members of the coloured communities in South Africa contributed – as well as the beginning of a new era of hope and promise.

South Africans have clamoured for decades for universal franchise – for one person, one vote in a single South Africa. The National Party took away the limited vote of African people in the Cape in 1936 and of coloured people in the Cape in 1956 by political manipulation. The franchise has been restored as a fundamental democratic right and everyone is now placed on the same rights footing. There is a mechanism which guarantees that those rights can never be removed again.

Democrats have yearned for every person to have equal protection under the law. For decades, coloured people were among those to suffer special abuses under apartheid laws – Group Areas and Mixed Marriages in particular – and as a result, did not experience the law as the guardian of their rights as citizens. Everyone must enjoy the right to be protected and not abused by the law.

Within this context, what are the real issues underlying the racial tensions in the Western Cape? Much has been made of identity issues. People are trying to reshape and reclaim their identities. This is healthy, and it should be encouraged. It is a search, an active process of re-claiming one's past.

However, in the process of trying to establish some form of identity, a number of points have been made of which we should take special note. The first is the danger of claiming an identity on the basis of putative racial boundaries – putative because there is actually no such thing as race. As a result of mass migrations and "mixing" over a long period of time, there is only one single human race. Secondly, people should be very careful about claiming identities on the basis of race because this can have consequences that lead to the break-up of states, genocide as well as igniting irrational and uncontrollable passions.

Is the tension about poverty and inequality? There are many poor people in this country and all residents have the responsibility to do something about it. But poor people are poor people. Coloured people do not stand ahead of Africans or Africans ahead of coloureds in the poverty queue. The Coloured Labour Preference clearly and powerfully discriminated against African people for a long time. But it is not clear that it benefited all coloured people as a group.

Is it about political representation then? Members of the coloured community have a promi-nent place in government. There is no statistical basis for claiming neglect on this score. All South Africans need to get involved in politics and creatively use politics for the benefit of all, not just some. There is room for better and greater representation. There is a leadership vacuum. Who leads and directs the communities of the Western Cape, particularly coloured ones? Are we training the next generation of leadership? Are we nurturing our political talents to create leaders of a calibre and sophistication that we can be proud of and trust? Are parties taking responsibility for this? Should we rely on parties to do it?

Is it about how people feel they are being treated or mistreated? How is the government treating coloured people? How are white people treating coloured people? How are African peo-ple treating coloured people? Let's turn the question around and ask how coloured people are treating whites and Africans and how they are responding to government? Do they treat all peo-ple, regardless of their colour, with the respect demanded of our Constitution? We also need to revisit our attitudes, to go through a process of spiritual renewal so that we treat others in the same manner as we expect them to treat us.

The point has been made, and needs to be emphasised, that people who come from the col-oured communities are not any more or any less racist than other communities. It is important to dispel that myth. Some people say coloured people have not yet entered the new South Africa and are particularly prone to using the racist language encouraged and tolerated under apartheid. But the phenomenon itself is not unique to sections of the coloured community. Racism is to be found in all spheres of our society – including the African sector – and it should be recognised as a national problem in search of a national solution.

In a society with a history where racism was the means of conducting interpersonal affairs and a valued commodity for some under apartheid oppression, none of this is surprising. It is also important to acknowledge that racism was used in the dominant white sectors as an instrument of power, and to a lesser extent in coloured and Indian communities to secure their intermediate position in the racial hierarchy constructed by apartheid that we have inherited.

But South Africans are now in a new moral and political order and we must get the axis right. We need to marshal our national spiritual and material resources in a visible campaign to combat expressions of racism – in the workplace, in our schools and in all aspects of our public life. The government alone cannot take on this problem. It needs the assistance of non-governmental or-ganisations and voluntary associations to give it life, and to reach the people who should be reached.

The second set of issues arising from this book relates to ambiguities in state strategies. It is not clear what precisely government strategy is in regard to both its general policies and its nation-building policies. Part of this lack of clarity has to do with government's inability to com-municate carefully with the attendant constituencies.

A second point about the ambiguities in state strategy has to do with what ordinary people are supposed to do when they believe they have been discriminated against in one form or another. There is confusion, unhappiness and frustration in the general population as people who believe that they have been discriminated against feel they cannot make claims to restitution.

President Mandela, in his opening address, said that if people believe they have been wronged and discriminated against, they must come to government. It is important that he made that call, but what we have is an incomplete set of infrastructures. Where would people go with this? They are supposed to go to the Human Rights Commission, according to its brief. This commission needs to be translated into a set of institutions and a set of practices that are accessible to people when they believe they have been wronged.

Every community in South Africa has concerns unique to their particular history and circum-stances. For the coloured communities of the Western Cape and elsewhere, perhaps the most pressing concern is the fear of being marginalised. It is a fear of a perceived continuation of a history where coloureds were used by whites to try and fragment the unity of liberation to where they now feel excluded from the benefits of a democratic order. It is a fear of being made to feel like perpetual losers.

If this fear is left unattended, it will undermine the very foundation of the democracy which South Africans have struggled so long to achieve. The papers that make up this book have not shied away from naming this fear and beginning to understand its source.

At the same time, people who make certain claims should be challenged on those claims. When ideas are offered, those ideas ought to be tested. The key is to have a commitment to democratic rules and democratic procedures. The danger is to translate certain points of view into areas of life and areas of activity that are not democratic – the danger of taking up arms, the danger of bullying, the danger of becoming hegemonic. The survival of this country depends on competition of ideas, competition over strategies – but where the rules of the game are accepted by all of us.

How then to approach the issue? Construing the politics of diversity as something to be "man-aged" is a tactic that leads us astray. The only acceptable concept is that of citizenship. This means we all have rights and that these are the same for everyone – including the rights to culture and language. We must claim the rights written into the Bill of Rights contained in the interim Constitution. And, importantly, we also have responsibilities and obligations tied to the exercise of those rights such as respect for others and treating others consistently with the rights we claim for ourselves. Racial and ethnic diversity must be guided by democratic principles. And we must teach our children these things. They are essential to peace, harmony and progress.

There is a need for a new partnership between the government and communities in South Africa in a spirit of reconciliation and renewal. The government should make clear its goals, plans and commitments, and should be sensitive to the marginality that people may experience or feel. All communities, including coloured communities, must embrace the new society and commit themselves to a process of nation building and a better life for all. ▲

Postscript:
June 1996

Kerry Cullinan

Since the publication of *Now That We Are Free* in South Africa, a number of significant political events have taken place that are either helping to build a common citizenship or show how far the country still has to go before all racial groups feel part of one nation.

The most important nation-building event was the adoption of the final Constitution, which commits the country to democracy, guarantees equality for all citizens, and recognises that "South Africa belongs to all who live in it, united in our diversity." The final Bill of Rights outlaws discrimination on the grounds of "race, gender, sex, pregnancy, marital status, ethnic or social origin, colour, sexual orientation, age, disability, religion, conscience, belief, culture, language and birth." This applies both vertically and horizontally, meaning that neither the state nor individuals may discriminate against anyone else on these grounds.

The Constitution also makes provision for the establishment of a number of institutions aimed at strengthening democracy. The last and most contentious commission to be agreed on by negotiators was the Commission for the Promotion and Protection of the Rights of Cultural, Religious and Linguistic Communities. The African National Congress (ANC) agreed during negotiations to set up this commission to accommodate the right-wing Freedom Front (FF), which is intent on Afrikaner self-rule. The commission's stated aims include promoting respect and tolerance for all the country's cultural, religious, and linguistic communities. The commission will also be able to recommend that "cultural councils" are established for a community, or communities.

While these terms of reference are rather vague, it is becoming clear that the commission has destructive as well as constructive potential. Senior ANC officials say that the commission marks a breakthrough in ANC thinking, as it is the first time that the party has acknowledged the existence of ethnic identities. But they also admit that they are worried that the commission will encourage various groups to mobilise on the basis of their ethnic differences—thus accentuating these differences, rather than promoting reconciliation.

ANC MP Yunus Carrim warns that "politicians who have a vested interest in mobilising ethnicity—those ethnic entrepreneurs—should as far as possible be excluded from participation in the commission" (*Mail & Guardian*, 24–30 May 1996). Both the FF and the National Party (NP) have claimed the commission as a victory. But senior Inkatha Freedom Party official Walter

Felgate has condemned the commission, describing it as an attempt by the ANC to control the ethnic debate.

The adoption of the final constitution on 8 May 1996 brought another twist to the nation-building project. A day after its adoption, the NP announced that it was withdrawing from the government of national unity as the ANC had failed to agree to entrench power sharing in the Constitution after 1999. The NP has since pledged itself to opposition politics, saying it aims to win over voters who have become disillusioned with the ANC. Senator David Malatsi, one of the NP's most senior African leaders, says that voting in South Africa at present is like conducting an "ethnic census." African people tend to vote for the ANC, while "minorities" vote mainly for the NP. The NP intended to break this mould by attracting supporters from all race groups, particularly African voters, he said.

But the most recent local government election, on 29 May 1996 in the Wester Cape, was certainly an "ethnic census." About 1.4 million voters in the Cape Town metropolitan area and 27 rural areas voted largely along racial lines. The NP failed to win a single ward seat in African townships in greater Cape Town; these were virtually all won by the ANC. At the same time, the NP generally swept the board in coloured townships.

People in Cape Town voted both directly for candidates in their residential wards and for parties to represent them at the two higher levels (equivalent to city and county levels in the United States). The NP won 48 percent of the party vote and the ANC won 38 percent. Support for the NP thus dropped 4 percent since the 1994 general election and increased by 2 percent for the ANC.

A number of disturbing racial incidents marred the election period. The most notable of these was when President Mandela was call a "kaffir" by NP supporters at a school in Mitchells Plain, a sprawling, working-class, coloured area built by the NP government to house coloured people it had removed from the inner city areas it had declared white. Ironically, Mandela had been viewing renovations to the school that he had personally asked a businessman to undertake.

The NP made no attempt to chastise its racist members. But Mandela's response was one of understanding. "I know they are victims of racist indoctrination and I have no hard feelings," he told a church gathering afterward. However, the incident shows that, despite Mandela's personal crusade to promote reconciliation between all racial and cultural groups, the process of building the nation still has a long way to go.

The elections also show that, increasingly, the NP is consolidating itself as the party that represents the interests of coloured people. This thought is repulsive to a number of coloured activists and academics who have been involved in the anti-apartheid struggle. A number of these people, however, also concede that the ANC has failed to take enough notice of the needs, fears, and aspirations of coloured communities. This has led to a proposal that a non-aligned "coloured movement" should be launched.

Trevor Oosterwyk, an ANC activist and history lecturer at the University of the Western Cape, is at the forefront of calls for a "coloured movement."

"I seems we will only begin to solve our problems [of NP domination of the Western Cape] if we are able to exert meaningful outside pressure on the ANC," Oosterwyk wrote in the *Cape Times* (19 February 1996) "In this regard, I feel that a new social movement among coloured activists is needed."

IIis proposal prompted a series of articles in the *Cape Times* from a variety of sources. The ANC's Western Cape chairperson, Chris Nissen, responded by saying: "For me, there is no doubt that the ANC provides a home for coloured people. The ANC has consistently shown a commitment to dealing with problems facing people on the ground. . . . We have all the statistics to show how many coloured communities have benefited from RDP projects, school feeding schemes, repairs to schools, free primary health care for children under six and the extension of municipal services" (*Cape Times*, 18 March 1996).

Mitchells Plain ANC leader Jerimia Thuynsma said he was not against the formation of a cultural organisation for coloured people. "Moves to form a coloured organisation to bring to the fore their different cultures should be welcomed," said Thuynsma (*Cape Times*, 18 April 1996). "Such an organisation is needed in this country. The coloured people are the only ones without a cultural organisation."

But, added Thuynsma, "the desire to form a new political party or movement to fight for the exclusive rights of coloured people could be most damaging to them and the country as a whole." The Western Cape secretary of the South African Communist Party, Phillip Dexter, said Oosterwyk's proposal to form a "coloured movement" was "profoundly disturbing," as it would simply "ghetto-ise coloured people in their 'own' organisations."

Thus the debate on where coloured communities fit into the new South Africa rages on unresolved in a situation where its resolution is crucial to nation building. In the coming months South Africans will no doubt take the debate further and with increased passion as the "minorities" commission and various cultural councils to take shape.   ▲

Index

MF, see Minority Front
Ministry of Public Service and
    Administration 74
Ministry of Trade and Industry 75
minorities 46-51
minority group 60-1
Minority Front (MF) 47, 49
multi-culturalism 111-13
multi-ethnicity 110-11
multiple identities 51
murder 16

N
Nactu, see National Council of Trade Unions
Natal Indian Congress (NIC) 47
National Agenda for Action 123
National Council of Trade Unions (Nactu) 26
national identity 2
National Institute for Crime Prevention and
    Rehabilitation of Offenders (Nicro) 17
National Manpower Commission report
    (1992) 86
National Party (NP) 135
    coloured support for 30-2, 36, 45, 46, 97
    coloured voters perceptions of 37
    credibility of intent of 41-2
    distribution of votes by community 45
    election campaign of 24-5, 29, 35-6,
        41-2, 55
    Indian support for 46
    swart gevaar tactics of 25, 35, 85
National Security Management System 25
national unity 2, 100-3, 104-7
    cost of in Brazil 128-9
nation-building 1, 72-3, 111, 115-16, 138
NIC, see Natal Indian Congress
Nicro, see National Institute for Crime
    Prevention and Rehabilitation of Offenders
Non-European Unity Movement 40, 95, 105-6
non-racialism 2, 6, 105-7
    and apartheid legacy 100-2
    definitions of 94-6
    fear of 57
    strategies for 102-3
NP, see National Party

O
October Household Survey (1994) 74
Operation Gangbust 17
'Opportunity 2000' 122

P
PAC, see Pan Africanist Congress
Pan Africanist Congress (PAC) 12, 39, 45
party identification 29-32
patronage 25
peer pressure 18
Police and Prisons Civil Rights Union
    (Popcru) 17

police corruption and complicity 17-18
political violence 15, 32, 48
Popcru, see Police and Prisons Civil Rights
    Union
political representation 136
politics of diversity 137
politics of identification 24
political stability 132
Pollsmoor 17
positive action 121-2
    examples of 122-3
    programme 122
positive discrimination 121
poverty 84-5, 136
power sharing 130-4
Presidential Lead Projects 6, 73
propaganda, power of 22-7, 35

R
race 64, 125
Race Relations Act (1976) 119-20
racial categorisation 64
racial discrimination 119-20
racial hierarchy 10-11, 14
racial identity 136
racial prejudices 48
racism 6-7, 10-11, 57, 64, 136-7
    in 1994 election 25-6, 42-3
    levels of 67-8
racist-inspired violence 25
rainbowism 89, 112
Rajbansi, Amichand 47, 49
RDP, see Reconstruction and Development
    Programme
RDP Fund 73
reconciliation 72-3
Reconstruction and Development Programme
    (RDP) 6, 12, 15, 18, 32, 84, 112, 115
    and affirmative action 72-6
    and nation building 72-3
    and reconciliation 72-3
    and role of the RDP Office 73-4
    and transformation of the civil service 74
resources, conflict over 11, 12-13, 50, 57
robbery 15, 16

S
San 56, 65
self-esteem 66
separate development 111-13
Sex Discrimination Act (1975) 120
skills shortages 78
'so-called' coloured people 41
socio-economic class, political support and
    34-6, 49
Sonn, Franklin 40
South African Police Services (SAPS) Gang
    Information Unit 16
Strategic Committee 25
Stratcom, see Strategic Committee

About the Institute for Democracy in South Africa (IDASA)

IDASA is an independent, public interest organisation committed to the promotion of democracy at all levels of South African society. It aims to promote and consolidate democracy and a culture of tolerance by designing and facilitating processes and programmes that transform institutions and empower individuals and communities as the basis for sustainable development in South Africa.

IDASA was founded at the end of 1986 to help find a democratic alternative to the politics of repression and to explore a new way of addressing the polarisation between black and white South Africans.

From the outset, IDASA emphasised that it was not a popular movement, nor a political party. It was committed to breaking down the fear and mistrust that divides South Africans and to bringing people together to talk and listen to each other in the creation of a true democracy.

The shifting South African political situation has implied important changes for IDASA. Much of the organisation's early work included facilitating meetings between members of then banned political organisations and prominent white South Africans. The aim was to help break down prejudices and misconceptions and find common ground.

However, since the unbanning of political organisations in 1990, and even more so since the democratic elections in 1994, the focus of IDASA's work has shifted to the creation of a democratic culture in South Africa and strategic interventions to help the new democracy take root and flourish.

The organisation hosts a variety of workshops, seminars, and training courses to promote the theory and practice of democracy at all levels of society. Key areas of activity include the development of good government, diversity, public safety, and security as well as the promotion of democratic citizenship.

IDASA's work is designed to encourage informed civilian participation in all aspects of social, economic, and political life. This involves, among other things, the organising of conferences and study tours as well as developing research projects and policy proposals. IDASA sees itself as a public interest organisation, committed to serving the public good.

IDASA produces a range of media to focus public attention on key issues that fall within the themes of the organisation's work. *Now That We Are Free* is one such publication. For more information contact IDASA's national office, P.O. Box 575, Rondebosch, Cape Town 7700, tel. (021)689-8389, fax (021)689-3261. ▲